clothesline
shed (lawnmower, bicycles,
cat cages
dog space, dog house
compost ? (in woods)
cold frame
screen house ? (in woods)
child's swing (in woods?)
sand box (patio or yard)
water pool
log pile
hibachi
see saw
tetherball
hammock
picnic table ?
badminton (in driveway)

A Book of Garden Plans

A BOOK OF
GARDEN PLANS

Muriel Stockdale Smith

PELHAM BOOKS

First published in Great Britain by
Pelham Books Ltd
52 Bedford Square,
London, W.C.1
1973

ISBN 0 7207 0665 3

Printed in Great Britain by
Western Printing Services Ltd Bristol
and bound by James Burn,
Esher, Surrey

To Frank
for all the happy years
of cheerful encouragement

Foreword

This is a book of ideas. It is aimed at setting the imagination to work before lifting the spade. It suggests not *how* but *where* to lay paving and plant trees and hedges: where to plan the outlines of flower and shrub borders and make room for a shed or swimming-pool.

The plans are drawn to varying scales to enable them to fit into the size of the page, but every plan has at least one measurement marked clearly and details can be gauged from this.

The same signs are used throughout. Roses are single hatched and shrubs cross hatched. Flower beds are left clear and paths, other than existing concrete or drives, are indicated as random squared paving.

I wish to thank all garden owners who have set me their problems and so made this book possible. Especially the Readers of the monthly magazine *Practical Gardening* and the Publishers for allowing me to make use of this material.

Grateful acknowledgement is made to Dagenham Landscapes and Warley Rose Gardens Ltd., who called me in to work on many of the Essex gardens.

Also my very sincere thanks to Mrs. Beryle Cornell who did all the typing for me.

M.S.S.
Boreham
Essex

Contents

Plans

Plan before you plant

All the plans in this book are for layouts of real garden sites. They give suggested solutions for the owner's individual problems. They are full of ideas which you may be able to adapt for part of your garden but they are not intended to be copied in their entirety. No two garden sites are exactly alike and it is this individuality which can give your garden its charm. Your garden should reflect your personality. Your likes and dislikes should show.

You probably spent a great deal of time measuring and viewing the rooms in your house from all angles. You spent hours choosing and rejecting various types of furniture and furnishings and the home now reflects your tastes and way of life.

With the garden, by the time you get round to dealing with it, there is usually little energy, time or money left. You take the line of least resistance and put in essentials, like a firm path from the back door to the clothes-line. You make, very hastily, a rough lawn and the rest of the garden develops as you acquire plants from neighbours or drop in container-grown plants from the garden centres, to give a quick colour effect. This method of attack is quite understandable but it does mean that you will find it twice as hard to change things later on, especially plants which have grown too large for their allotted positions. The layout—or a member of the family—will always be nagging at you because the garden is not really convenient and therefore irritating in its failure to be a worth-while extension of the home. It has not developed into a place which all the family can use as an extra room in which to enjoy their many varied hobbies and activities.

CHOOSING YOUR SITE

Start right at the beginning. If you have any choice, give some thought to the aspect of the garden and its immediate surroundings when you are choosing your house. On a newly developing estate, you might be able, by a little forethought, to avoid, for example, choosing the site where the garden will be in deep shadow from the house from afternoon onwards, just the time of day when you and the returning family might want to enjoy being out in the evening sunlight. Naturally, the aspect of your rooms will come first but also keep in mind the garden aspect. Space on the north side of the house may be a dead loss as far as gardening is concerned. Space on the south side might be developed into a real feature of the garden.

TAKING A DETACHED LOOK

Once you have moved into a house it is very difficult to take a detached look at your outdoor surroundings. If it is a new site you are bothered by the mounds of rubble and sub-soil left by the builders. If it is an established garden, a special tree or blaze of colour takes your eye and you can't see how to set about altering things to suit your requirements. The best way to clear your mind of all these complications is to get the boundaries, house and essential details down on to paper.

Before your house was built, a plan was drawn up. All the constructional details were down on paper so that the builder had an over-all picture of what the finished house would look like. In the same way, if you can find the time and patience to work out a complete plan for the sort of garden you want, if possible before you lift a spade or lay the first paving stone, you will save yourself endless frustration, time, energy, money and disappointment.

MAKING THE PLAN

Before you start to think that you are no good at drawing, I suggest you acquire a large sheet of graph paper. Most stationers stock these in various sizes and scales. With a ruler and pencil you can then draw out the measurements of your site, without worrying at all about free-hand drawing.

With the deeds of your house you will probably find a scaled sketch giving the boundary measurements, and if yours is a new house you probably have also a builder's site and house plan with detailed measurements. If neither of these is available it means measuring for yourself, with a tape measure and the help of a friend. If all else fails, pace the boundaries out for yourself, knowing that an average good stride is roughly three feet. Measure the house, making a careful note of the position of downstair doors and windows. If you jot these figures down on a rough piece of paper as you go round the garden you can then transfer them to the graph paper in comfort, indoors. Mark carefully the width and position of any really permanent paths. Any manholes or large trees—anything which you can't or don't want to move. Mark in the aspect of the garden—the north point—because this will have a good deal to do with the layout planning. Make a note of the type of boundaries; hedges, closed fencing or wiring. Any distant views you want to keep or eyesores you want to blot out. Make a note, and be thankful for, any variations in levels. Use can be made of these to give more interest to your garden than is normally possible on a flat site.

If you are dealing with an old, overgrown garden, ignore at the moment the position of rose beds, ungainly borders, uneven grass paths through vegetable gardens and delapidated rockwork. With just the essential details down on your graph paper you will be able to look at your site with fresh eyes, dealing only with the things that are there to stay.

If you finally go over all these lines with a ball-point or felt-tipped pen you will have a permanent, basic plan on which to work with pencil and rubber, or you may prefer to work on a piece of tracing paper laid over the basic plan.

DESIGNING YOUR OWN GARDEN

Now is the time to let your imagination run riot. Visit all the gardens you can to stimulate your ideas. Study pictures of old historical gardens as well as modern ones. All designs which have survived have evolved from the needs of the people who used them. If your design grows out of your needs it will be functional, satisfying and beautiful. Think of your garden as an extension to your home, and plan what use you would like to make of it. It will help to make an actual list of your requirements. These will vary according to the household.

Those with a young or growing family will want, among other things:

A clean, hard surface near the kitchen and living room doors, to give plenty of room for movement.

A firm path to a clothes line or drier.

Gates where necessary, for safety reasons.

Plenty of clear lawn space.

A sand pit, which might later become a pool.

A rough play area, screened from the main flower garden.

Vegetable, soft fruit and salad areas.

Somewhere for pets.

Shallow and not too numerous steps.

Those planning for retirement would probably start the list with:

'Sitting out' places and at least one permanent seat, preferably with a view across the garden, rather than the view seen from the house windows.

As much privacy as possible, without hedges needing constant trimming.

Extra buildings such as sun room, greenhouse and ample shed space.

Raised beds and planting in trough walls.

Rose beds of manageable proportions.

Perennials in island beds, for easy maintenance.

Trees and shrubs to give permanent background and interest at all seasons of the year.

Water, in some form.

ALLOCATING THE AREAS

With your list as a guide you will be able to think of your garden in areas and start to rough in sections on your graph paper. You might even like to have small scraps of paper labelled vegetables, play area, rose beds, shrub borders and patio, for example, and move these around on your outline plan, rather like a jigsaw puzzle, until you have a good arrangement, based on the aspect of your plot.

Start with the house doors and plan access to a patio or sitting out place, where it will get sunshine at the time of day when you, or your family, are free to enjoy it. No garden is really an extension of your home unless the design includes space for a permanent seat. If you arrange a sheltered spot you will be surprised how much use you can make of a garden seat from January to December, even with, or because of, our fickle climate. If the seat is there, you will use it. If you have to take out temporary garden furniture you won't bother. Friends will appreciate your garden much more if you can extend to them the same courtesy as you would to house visitors.

By careful planning, the path which gives access to your sitting out place can also serve to give access to the clothes line or drier, and link with the vegetable garden or children's play area. On the way it may form a walk between rose or flower borders, or wind amongst shrubs or orchard trees. Such careful designing means that the paths —the backbone of your garden—will be unobtrusive, yet strictly functional.

Once you have decided on the actual areas for the various garden features you want to include, you can get down to smaller details. For example, do you want immediate privacy with a closed fence, or are you content to sacrifice some of the width of your garden and wait a little longer for a hedge or a line of cordon fruit to grow?

When you are working out the details of paths, borders and steps, check that you have pleasing proportions. For example, there should be width if possible between twin borders for two people to walk together comfortably. This doesn't mean, necessarily, a wide, hard path. A grass walk, with flagstones as a central strip may be all that is needed. A terrace or sitting out place should be large enough to take your garden furniture easily. Try spacing the pieces out on the site. You will be surprised how much room garden chairs really need. Most garden steps are made too narrow and skimpy, and often too steep. Groups of two or three steps with a landing are far more gracious than a single flight.

One main place from which to check your proposed design is from the house windows. For many months of the year this will be your main view of the garden. Untrue angles and wiggly lines will be irritating and look untidy. If paths and borders are based on the angles of the house, the outline of your garden will be pleasing and restful even on the greyest winter day. If your house has picture windows you tend to become so used to the main view of the garden that it soon seems to lack any element of mystery. Shrub borders can be placed where the varied shapes of the planting can enhance or frame the view all the year round. Try to arrange the planting so that there are focal points across the garden for you to enjoy once you are outside, as a change from the ever present view from your window.

WORKING OUT THE PLAN

When you feel you have everything worked out, go into the garden and mark out the line of your paths and beds and borders with some stout pegs and string. This way you will be able to check on the proportions and know that everything will fit into the overall boundaries. If you have arranged for curved borders, make sure that you have a clear outline, based definitely on part of a circle and not just a wavy wandering line. By attaching pegs to the right length of string, and using one as a compass point, you can mark out an accurate curve on the soil, finally defining the outline with permanent pegs. If you want to cut out a border or island bed on an existing lawn, you can get a good curve by walking round the proposed outline with the mower. This way you will know that you are not making awkward curves for future lawn cutting. On a bare sight, you might like to lay a hose pipe flat and shape it into the curve you want, before inserting pegs.

Once you are satisfied with the actual layout measurements on the site, it is probably worth while filling in the details on your basic graph plan in ink. This will give you a permanent working drawing. Then you can go ahead with whichever part of the garden is most urgent for your immediate enjoyment, without any feeling of rush or hurry. Once you have this picture of the overall plan in your mind's eye you will be able to enjoy the garden-making step by step, knowing that everything is working towards the final effect you want. You may adapt or alter some features as the family and circumstances change—it depends how long you take over the job—but at least you will be saved any major upheavals or disappointments.

THINKING ABOUT PLANTING

Through all your planning, the type of plants you want to grow will have been at the back of your mind. That border is for roses; here you want shrubs; your special chrysanthemums would do well there. It is a great temptation to outline the borders and rush in the planting before giving yourself time for careful soil preparation. The main planting season for nursery stock such as trees, shrubs, fruit trees, roses and most perennials is roughly from September to March. With a new garden, aim at preparing the sites and planting the larger permanent material such as ornamental trees, fruit trees and shrubs during these months, then they can be getting established and growing on. This is where you reap the benefit of your garden plan. There is little danger of your wanting to move these matured plants at a later date.

Should you happen to move in spring and miss the main planting season, use a line of runner beans or sweet peas to take the place of a hedge for the first summer. Use annuals and bedding plants to give a quick colour effect without interfering with your basic border preparations for the early autumn.

If you really want an immediate effect you can use container-grown plants. You will have to be prepared for constant care and watering during the summer months, but 'instant' gardening can be fun, although more expensive than traditional slow cultivation.

Most gardeners plant flowering shrubs too closely together. You can space them out and fill the bare spaces with large bays of perennials such as lupins, or bedding plants such as petunias or Coltness dahlias, to give you summer colour during the first few seasons. Or you can plant the shrubs closer together, and move some of them out in a few years time to other borders as you have time to prepare them.

If you want to experiment with growing shrubs from cuttings, or raising biennials and perennials from seed, grow them in rows in a slightly shaded part of the garden, perhaps a part of the vegetable plot. Name them clearly and let them grow on undisturbed. Here, they will not be forgotten or overlooked. Cuttings and odd sowings mixed up in the main borders are easily forgotten and damaged and they hinder the general clean up of borders in the autumn.

Keep your ink master plan by you, perhaps mounted on card; you will be able to make a record of your planting schemes on it. Details for example of the varieties of roses and shrubs planted will help you with your pruning.

WORK ON THE SITE

It is difficult to say which is the more bewildering, to be faced with a new site covered with mounds of sub-soil and builder's rubbish, or an old garden rank with nettles and cluttered with overgrown shrubs and broken paths.

After an initial clearance of any large rubbish, it might be worth considering buying, or hiring, a powered tool to turn the soil and help clear buried rubbish. If you feel this task is beyond you or the time you have available, it is possible to hire an operator with the tool. He can make a transformation in a few hours, clearing and re-arranging the levels as he works, to your requirements, based on your proposed layout. From your plan you will know where your main borders are to be and so you can make sure that sub-soil is not dumped there but re-buried or spread around where paths or paved areas are intended. In about two hours a skilled man with a powered tool can do the work it would take the garden owner many weekends to do with hand tools. The site is then ready for the owner to deal with the more exciting details of garden making, like shaping beds and borders or sowing or turfing lawns.

A layout plan comes in useful again if there is some special part of the work such as walling, paving or steps with which the owner would like some help from a skilled garden contractor. With identical tracings of the part of the garden under consideration the owner can get accurate alternative estimates for the work. It is always worth while getting two written estimates for comparison. Before you accept an estimate it might be worth seeing the contractor's work in another garden. Usually, he is only too pleased to show you. This is an extra precaution, in addition to a friend's verbal recommendation. If you want help with constructional or large planting work it is wise to think about it as early as August or September. The contractor will be free to give your job his full attention, agree on estimates and get started on the work before any snowy weather sets in. If you wait till the first flush of gardening enthusiasm in the spring, he will be overwhelmed with work, and the best season for permanent planting will slip away.

In autumn, the nurseryman will be able to reserve any particular plant varieties you select and will deliver them at the best planting time. Later on, you will find you have to accept substitutes.

From a purely practical point of view, we know that any work undertaken in the garden increases the value of the property. At the same time, we are all becoming aware of the great value of the garden as a place for relaxation and recreation. We are often warned that the pattern of our working lives is altering and we must plan for greater leisure time.

The problem seems to be that people seeking recreation, all tend to want to be in the same places at the same times on the same days. We all know the frustrations of crowded weekend roads and packed beaches, sports areas and beauty spots. One answer is to make wiser use of our own gardens.

At the end of the book are several designs, for large and small gardens, planned to give room for all the family to enjoy leisure pastimes. Today, swimming pools, games lawns and children's areas, sheltered patios and settings for barbecues are taking the place of large, walled fruit and vegetable gardens and vast conservatories. This emphasis on planning for leisure enjoyment, under your own control, in your own garden, makes good sense for adults and children.

I hope you will find something among these plans to set your imagination working and help you to find health and refreshment in creating a garden which will be a constant satisfaction and joy to you, your family, your visitors and friends and passers by.

1 Looking at your plot

The move is over. The house is more or less straight, so now you feel you can take time off to look at the garden. It may be a new, bare site or it may be an overgrown wilderness, but if this is the first time you have really looked at it you might be in for some nasty shocks.

What about aspect? Does the house shade most of the garden from midday onwards? Are your neighbour's tall trees on your north or south boundary? Unalterable facts like these are going to make all the difference to the sort of garden you can create.

Mention to people that you are interested in gardening and they will immediately begin to talk about plants. Yet a house is described by its overall size and the arrangement of its rooms, not the colour of the furnishings. Flowers, trees and shrubs are the things which furnish a garden once you have decided how to arrange the space at your disposal. If you start with the basic shape of the plot and think in terms of space and structures first and furnishings afterwards, you will avoid costly mistakes and a lot of unnecessary maintenance work once the garden is laid out and planted. Of course, at the back of your mind as you plan you know the types of plants you want to grow and you will be arranging to give them the best possible positions and conditions under which to thrive.

As you look at your plot from all angles, and through the house windows, notice the things which can give your garden individuality. Let the shape and existing features inside and outside the boundaries dictate your arrangements. Work with your site and develop all its possibilities from the start. Time spent thinking and dreaming about it now may seem a waste of time but will bring more lasting satisfaction. Especially if you have taken over an established, or neglected garden, take time to see a season's growth round. You may discover plant treasures or find out, in winter time, why a tree was planted to screen that exact spot.

Notice any changes in levels, however slight, any moist corners or very dry sunbaked areas.

Notice which parts are overlooked by neighbouring windows.

Have a good look at your own house and decide what type of garden and planting will enhance it. Thinking on these lines you will gradually build up a picture of what can be achieved on your own site to bring out its individuality.

Choosing a site

Not many householders have a chance to make a choice of sites these days, but if you are able to indulge in the luxury of comparing alternative plots it is worth studying various features.

The position of a house just round the bend of the road, or on the opposite side, will affect the quota of sunshine and wind protection the garden receives. On this estate plan the rear of Plot A, for example, will get little afternoon sun, while the rear of Plots D and E will be real suntraps.

Any existing trees, as long as they are not large, overgrown forest types, can be used to give immediate character to the layout. This is especially true if you acquire a segment of woodland or a site on part of an old garden. The trees on Plot C make an interesting group and give shade only in late afternoon, while Plot H would be deprived of all morning sunshine. Also this larger house would keep western sun away from the small rear garden. Plot F would benefit from the siting of the three trees, but Plot G might find them rather a nuisance, from a planning point of view.

The position of the house on the plot also affects your gardening possibilities. If you are a plantsman, you may like to be well back from the road with most of the garden on show. Or you may prefer a larger secluded garden at the rear. Room at the side of a house can be very useful, but a corner site can be a perpetual worry and irritation.

This estate layout has open plan front gardens. The wide sweeps of lawn give a restful and neighbourly appearance and means little work for the owners. To give privacy to the rear gardens, the expense of fencing or walling would have to be considered.

Uneven sites usually mean expenditure on constructional materials,

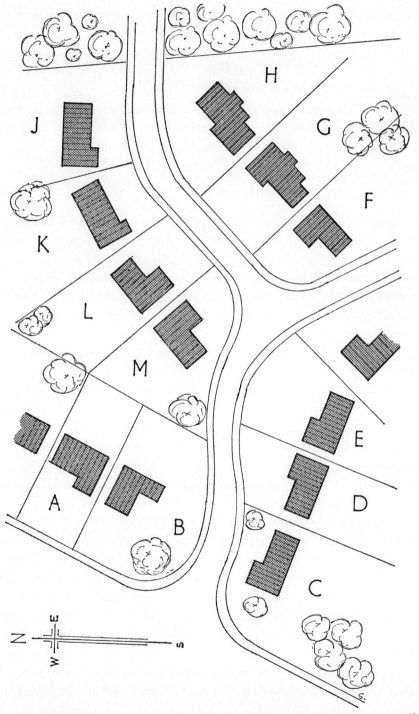

but they can often be adapted to make the garden more interesting than is possible on a flat site. They are a worth-while challenge.

Soil is another consideration. It can be refreshing to have to learn about plants to suit your particular soil, but if you really want to grow just rhododendrons and heaths, for example, it is wise to try and avoid choosing a site on the chalk downs. Every site has its own difficulties and delights, and offers scope for individual skill in planning a garden to suit the owners needs and tastes.

No two sites are identical

Two garden plots 32 ft x 76 ft at the rear of houses of the same type on an estate would seem to have the same problems. Yet each has individual assets and difficulties. Add to these the varying needs of the householders, and the final layouts can be totally different.

Right from the start, the question of aspect makes a difference to the use which will be made of the door leading from the living-room to the garden.

Garden A will get morning sunshine here so the area will be used quite often and, as there is a young family, the paving is extended to give a clear patio space to catch the sunshine for longer periods.

The door to garden B faces north and will be little used, so planting is brought right round so that it can be enjoyed by those sitting in the house, especially as this is to be lived in by an older couple whose family have grown up.

A hedge is planted on part of the central division, and both plots have close-boarded fencing on the other boundaries.

Garden A has flower borders to soften the outline of the patio as it meets the lawn, which is kept open and uncluttered to allow for ball games. A path leads from the patio, past climbers on the north boundary fence, to give direct access to a summer house. Here there is an area of rough grass, solely for children's enjoyment. It is screened from the main lawn by a shrub border. A small flowering tree gives a little shade here, and screens an alternative entrance to the children's area.

In later years this sunny area could be developed as a rose, or rock and water garden. A border for flowers could also be added, to

GARDEN 'A' | GARDEN 'B'

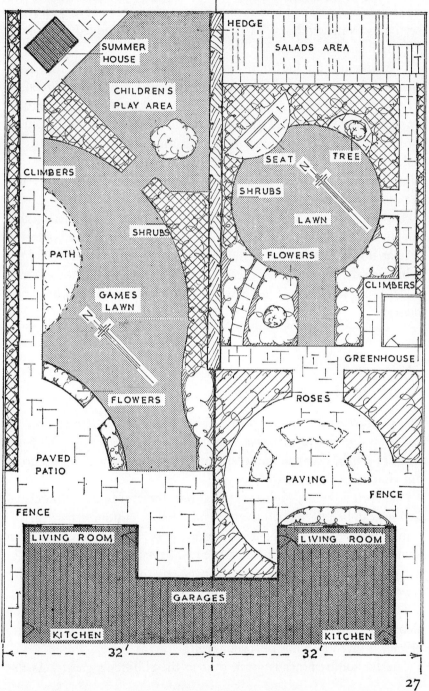

GARDEN 'A'

- SUMMER HOUSE
- CHILDREN'S PLAY AREA
- CLIMBERS
- SHRUBS
- PATH
- GAMES LAWN
- FLOWERS
- PAVED PATIO
- FENCE
- LIVING ROOM
- KITCHEN
- 32'

GARDEN 'B'

- HEDGE
- SALADS AREA
- SEAT
- TREE
- SHRUBS
- LAWN
- FLOWERS
- CLIMBERS
- GREENHOUSE
- ROSES
- PAVING
- FENCE
- LIVING ROOM
- KITCHEN
- 32'

GARAGES

soften the straight line of the paved path. In garden B, a squared-off paved area is developed as a formal rose garden, pleasant as seen from the living-room windows. Extra rose beds could be added if the area is not to be used too much for sitting out.

A greenhouse on the south boundary is flanked by a paved path which leads to a small salad-growing area at the end of the garden.

From the paved rose garden, a wide grass walk opens into a circular lawn. Flowers screen out the base of the greenhouse, while shrub borders give privacy to a seat, set facing south on a paved recess. To make for easier maintenance, the shrub border screening out the salad area is cut into by a circle of paving with a small flowering tree in the centre.

Planting near the paved rose garden is also made more manageable and interesting by a curved walk, giving an alternative way onto the circular lawn. Another small flowering tree might be introduced here to balance the height of the greenhouse, as seen from the house. Once made, this garden would need very little upkeep, yet is full of varied interest.

An awkward corner site
LYMINGTON, HAMPSHIRE

The position of the house on this corner plot cuts the garden area up into several rather unattractive sections. There is also a slight fall from south to north, near the house so that the existing terrace stands up in full view from the side roadway.

It is certainly an awkward site, but these seemingly unrelated sections can be put to good use to make a practical, family garden.

In houses, the open plan arrangement of living-rooms has been found by many families to be restless. The same principles apply in the garden, and it can be more convenient to have odd corners for various activities than to be able to see the whole garden at a glance.

The vegetable garden drops neatly and unobtrusively into the section along the side road boundary. There is a closed fence here, but extra privacy is given by a line of cordon fruit.

The far south corner is given over to the children's games. As this

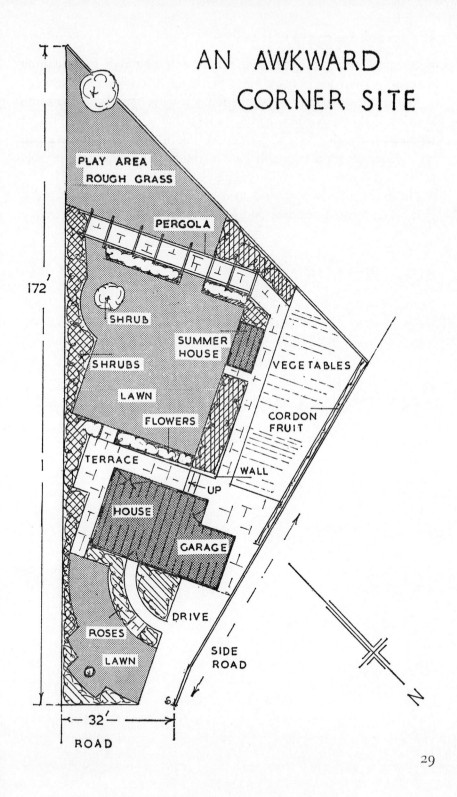

AN AWKWARD CORNER SITE

PLAY AREA
ROUGH GRASS

PERGOLA

172'

SHRUB

SHRUBS

SUMMER
HOUSE

VEGETABLES

LAWN

CORDON
FRUIT

FLOWERS

TERRACE

WALL

UP

HOUSE

GARAGE

DRIVE

ROSES

SIDE
ROAD

LAWN

N

32'

ROAD

29

is screened out by a pergola it can be left as rough grass without detracting from the outlook from the house windows.

As the terrace is so exposed, the main lawn is bounded by screening shrub and flower borders, and a summer house is included. This has its back to the side road and faces full south. It is reached by a path which also serves the vegetable garden and leads on, under the pergola, to give dry access to the children's play area.

The front garden is planted as a rose garden, with beds shaped to give access to the front door and round to the south side of the terrace.

2 Working out a plan

Most people have some idea of the sort of garden they would like to own. They think of vivid flower or rose planting in formal beds, with razor-sharp edges to the immaculate lawn. Or a trim patio, gay with planted bowls and vases, and a fountain jet splashing in the background. Or a rock and water garden leading to woodland walks through massed banks of azaleas. Perhaps all they want is a garden with flowers everywhere, allowed to grow and seed at will.

Then they look out of the window at the new, bare plot, still littered with builder's debris or the unrelated paths and planting left by the previous owner. It all seems hopeless. The line of least resistance is to tidy it up and lay turves, or sow a lawn, and leave a narrow border for planting on three sides. The result is a layout you can see at a glance and it is just like hundreds of other gardens.

It takes quite a lot of hard work to make even a dull garden like this, and it still has to be maintained.

However small your plot is, you can, by thinking about it and using imagination, create a living picture which will serve the needs of you and your household, and be a constant joy.

The secret is to think about the whole layout—before you even lift a spade. Plan before you plant. Start by making a written list of the things you really need. This might include a shed, a clothes drier, dry paving near the house and a lawn. Then add to the list all the things you would like to have. Rose beds, trees and shrubs, alpines, a summer house, an informal pool and so on.

In the introduction you will find details of how to work these requirements into a plan drawn on graph paper. Start on the adventure of making a working drawing which you can use and adapt for as many years as you live in that house, eventually turning your pipe dreams into reality.

The plans in this chapter show practical examples of actual sites and how their problems were tackled.

Allocation of areas
NEW MILTON, HAMPSHIRE

One way of sorting out ideas is to make a list of all the features needed in the garden. Then they can be roughed in on the graph plan, or even written on slips of paper and moved around according to aspect and ease of access. Once these main areas are settled, the details will fall into place. This is a very helpful way of dealing with a bare, new site.

The list made by the owner of this new detached house was:

1. Privacy from upper windows of the neighbouring two houses.
2. A more direct approach to the front door.
3. Somewhere for fruit and vegetables.
4. A greenhouse.
5. A pleasant outlook from the sun room and main windows.
6. An informal pool.
7. A formal rose garden.
8. Trees, shrubs and flowers.

Looking at his site plan, the obvious place for the greenhouse and fruit and vegetables seemed to be behind the garage where he could link these with the drive and the paths serving the side doors.

Trees and shrubs could be used to screen out the houses and also form a background to the informal pool. This is set in paving to make for ease of maintenance and enhanced by low shrub planting and a small flowering tree, with the screening trees rising behind.

An opening is cut in the front boundary hedge for a paved path, linking the paved terrace by the front door and the formal rose garden. The paved terrace is extended to give plenty of room for movement outside the sun room, and then turns along the east side of the house to link with the fruit and vegetable garden. An arch and a line of cordon fruit screen these utility areas from the lawn and flower beds outline the paved terrace for colour and scent near the house windows.

In the rose garden, a seat facing south has a view of the curved grass walk leading between the screen boundary planting and the pool. This helps to detract from the squareness of the plot. The outline of the boundary planting borders allows room for bold groupings of perennial plants where they will give colour as seen from the sun room.

The expanse of the drive is softened by a corner border of flowering shrubs to allow room for a small flowering tree.

NEW SITE — ALLOCATION OF AREAS

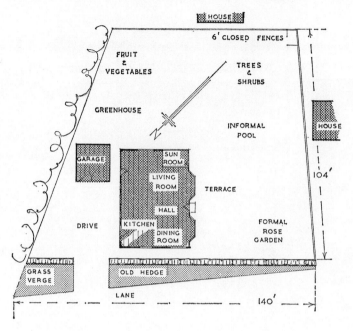

FINAL LAYOUT

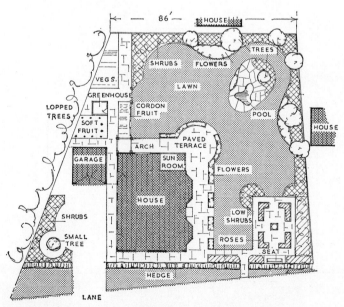

33

LAYOUT OF EXISTING GARDEN

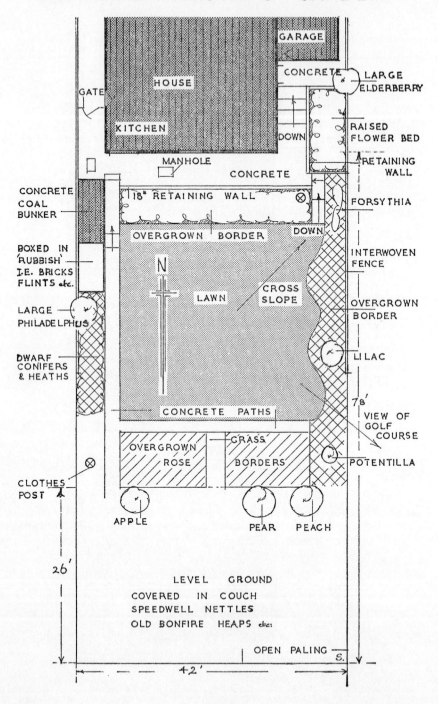

GARAGE

CONCRETE

LARGE
ELDERBERRY

HOUSE

GATE

KITCHEN

DOWN

RAISED
FLOWER BED

RETAINING
WALL

MANHOLE

CONCRETE

CONCRETE
COAL
BUNKER

18" RETAINING WALL

FORSYTHIA

OVERGROWN BORDER

DOWN

INTERWOVEN
FENCE

BOXED IN
'RUBBISH'
I.E. BRICKS
FLINTS etc.

N

CROSS
SLOPE

LAWN

OVERGROWN
BORDER

LARGE
PHILADELPHUS

LILAC

DWARF
CONIFERS
& HEATHS

CONCRETE PATHS

78'

VIEW OF
GOLF
COURSE

OVERGROWN
ROSE

GRASS
BORDERS

POTENTILLA

CLOTHES
POST

APPLE

PEAR   PEACH

26'

LEVEL   GROUND
COVERED   IN COUCH
SPEEDWELL NETTLES
OLD BONFIRE HEAPS etc.

OPEN PALING

S.

42'

THE BASIC PLAN

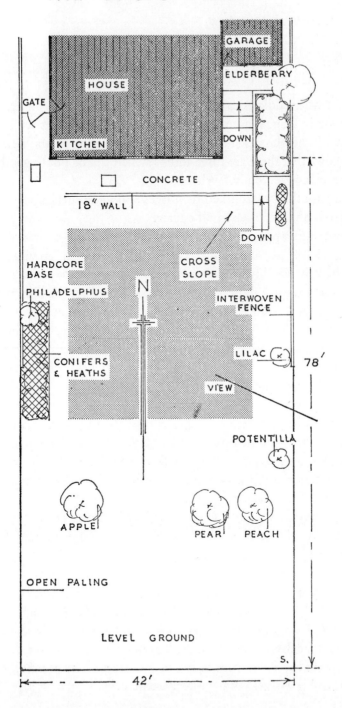

A garden alteration
WOODMANSTERNE, SURREY

The plan on the previous page, giving the layout of an existing garden, indicates all the problems and difficulties. The best way to deal with this sort of muddle is to get essential details down on paper.

The Basic Plan, ignores everything except the features which cannot be altered and those which it is worth considering in the new layout. This shows that there are three things which can be put to good use:

There is a variation in levels.

There are three established fruit trees and some shrubs.

There is a view across a golf course.

Opposite this page is The New Layout. A general clearance involves getting rid of the unwanted coal bunker and an accumulation of rubbish. It is possible to remove the decrepit concrete paths, so there is now a chance for a more informal layout, based on the distant view.

The removal of the coal bunker allows room for an extension to the concrete area, forming a sun-trap corner, with flower beds in front of the extended retaining wall. Soil from this corner is used to build up the north-east corner of the sloping lawn into a flower bed, level with the existing concrete.

The steps on this side of the garden are retained and a paved path leads from them, past a flower border with a background of shrubs. The path turns south, between two of the existing fruit trees, to lead to a shed and the fruit and vegetable garden. The other fruit tree now stands out as a specimen on the lawn, backed by the rearranged rose beds which screen out the vegetable garden.

The shrub border on the west boundary is curved out so that it helps to frame the view across the lawn to the golf course, as seen from the new, curved steps. Planting in this border is kept low on the south side of the greenhouse. This is sited near the house as it is intended for the display of a cactus collection, as well as general routine use.

An island bed for low shrub planting also helps to frame the main view and screens the line of the paved path. A movable clothes drier replaces the existing clothes posts. It is planned to work on this garden over a period of from three to five years, and so have a useful, practical and restful garden in time for retirement.

36

THE NEW LAYOUT

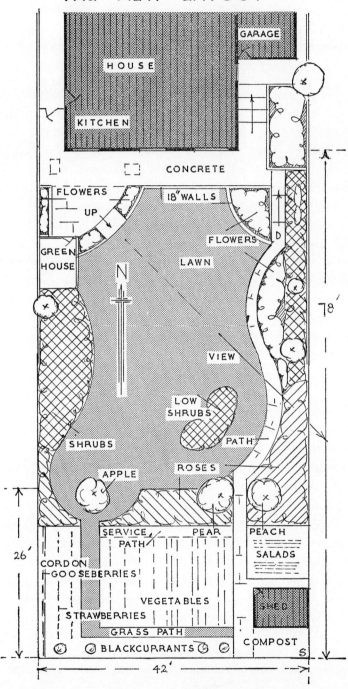

Linking house and garden
NEW MALDEN, SURREY

Ideally, the garden should make the perfect setting for the house. House and garden form one unit. Doors should relate to garden paths, and windows to garden views. Although this is often forgotten, the views from the garden back to the house are also important.

This harmony is only achieved by thinking about the textures and colours of plant and constructional material chosen. We have all seen vivid coloured paved paths leading up to bright red brick houses and weeping willow trees planted outside picture windows.

House doors form the direct link with the garden. Don't be satisfied with the narrow concrete paths most builders put round the house. Kitchen and living-room doors require room for movement round them if tempers and grass edgings are not to be frayed.

This house is placed awkwardly on the plot for easy access to the garden. The problem has been solved by combining rear and side garden in a wide circular arrangement of rose beds, based on the kitchen door. With children, the inner circle should be paved but the retired couple for whom this was planned, preferred to bring grass as close as possible to the house. The rose beds are, however, backed by paving to make for easy maintenance.

Most windows of the house have a view of this rose garden feature, and its neatness makes a pleasant contrast with the existing woodland on the far boundary.

Woodland like this seems to have great possibilities but it can develop into a worrying, untidy mess. The main thing is to give it some sort of shape. It may be possible to run a mower through occasionally, keeping open rough grass tracks. If it is damp, large flagstones can take the place of grass. This way it will seem part of the garden layout and not look too untidy. Some low ground cover planting, flanking the outlines of the tracks will give colour and foliage to screen out coarser growth or bare soil under the trees.

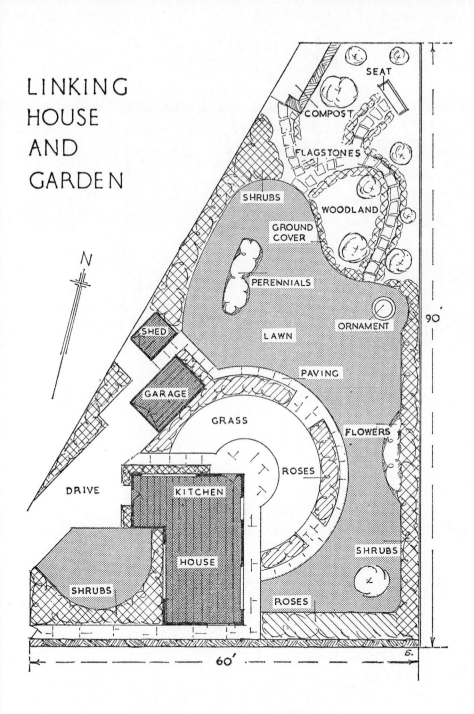

LINKING
HOUSE
AND
GARDEN

N

SEAT

COMPOST

FLAGSTONES

SHRUBS

GROUND COVER

WOODLAND

PERENNIALS

ORNAMENT

SHED

LAWN

GARAGE

PAVING

GRASS

FLOWERS

ROSES

DRIVE

KITCHEN

SHRUBS

HOUSE

ROSES

SHRUBS

90'

60'

S.

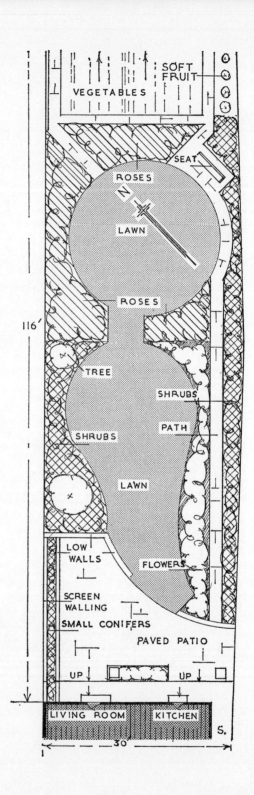

SOFT
FRUIT

VEGETABLES

SEAT

ROSES

N

LAWN

ROSES

TREE

SHRUBS

PATH

SHRUBS

LAWN

116'

LOW
WALLS

FLOWERS

SCREEN
WALLING

SMALL CONIFERS

PAVED PATIO

UP

UP

LIVING ROOM

KITCHEN

S.

30

40

3 Shapes and sizes

My garden is such an odd shape I don't know where to begin. Mine is so long and narrow I can't think how to make it interesting. These are often the first reactions of owners to their new garden plots. Yet if the site can be approached with an open mind and not too many preconceived ideas, the shape and size of the plot will help to stimulate ideas for its design. Keeping in mind the proportions of the site and its relationship to the house will help to ensure a balanced, functional garden layout.

There was a time, in the days of ribbon development, when the vast majority of gardeners had to cope with small, or even tiny front gardens and long, thin back gardens, probably thirty feet or less in width. Now, with infilling and the development of new estates, garden plots are any shape and size and on any level. With houses being built on any available site, and land at any angle to the house, garden owners are being faced with exciting problems. There is great scope for individuality. House buyers have come to expect their homes to be fully equipped, leaving little for the do-it-yourself enthusiast to enjoy. Now the garden can become the great challenge to the imagination of the owner and his craftsmanship.

A long garden
HEXTABLE, KENT

The patio outside this semi-detached house is shaped to allow for it catching the maximum sunshine. A rectangular bed for low planting helps to disguise a manhole cover, and the awkward levels down from the kitchen and living-room doors.

For privacy, low walls outline the shape of the patio, leaving a wide opening on to the main lawn. The low wall continues down the north boundary to form a trough border for small conifer planting, backed by screen walling. Narrow borders could replace the walls with much the same effect of privacy.

A paved path, giving direct access to the fruit and vegetable garden, runs between shrub planting on the south boundary and a curved flower border on the lawn side. This gives colour and privacy as seen from the patio.

Shrubs and a flowering tree give privacy along the north boundary and help to form an unusual shape to the main lawn. This widens out into a circular rose garden, thus breaking up the length of the plot while still retaining an open view of most of the site.

A seat, set in the rose garden on a paved recess, faces west, and catches the afternoon sunlight denied to the patio. Paths make for easy management of the rose borders and the extensive fruit and vegetable garden.

Small rectangular site
ILFORD, ESSEX

A narrow path going right up the garden accentuates the long, narrow, closed fence outlines of this plot behind a terrace house.

As the house faces south, the existing concrete outside the kitchen door is extended in a quarter circle, from which to enjoy the view across the garden, instead of straight up it. Part of the old path is removed to allow for an informal lawn, flanked by flower and shrub borders.

The remaining path, towards the south boundary, is enlarged as two semi-circles, allowing room for gay bedding flowers.

A curved shrub border on the east boundary helps to screen out the existing shed, and also makes a recess for a seat, with a view westwards, across the garden to curved, boundary flower borders. The two existing apple trees make a background to this formal part of the garden, as viewed from the informal lawn.

The whole plot is only twenty feet wide by sixty feet long, and the alterations create a lot of interest in quite a small garden.

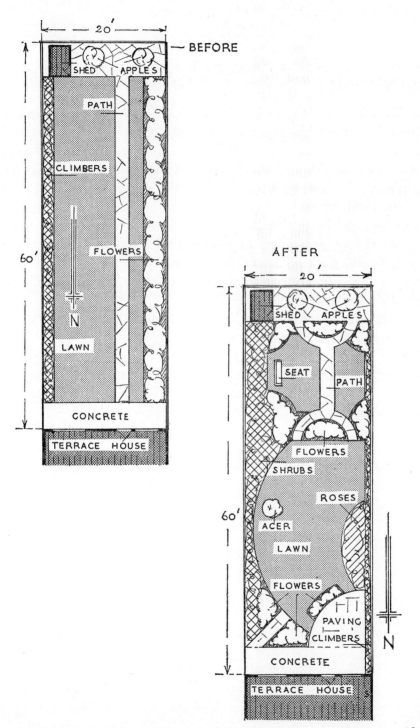

BEFORE

20'

SHED   APPLES

PATH

CLIMBERS

FLOWERS

N

LAWN

CONCRETE

TERRACE HOUSE

60'

AFTER

20'

SHED   APPLES

SEAT

PATH

FLOWERS

SHRUBS

ROSES

ACER

LAWN

FLOWERS

PAVING

CLIMBERS

N

CONCRETE

TERRACE HOUSE

60'

43

Garage outside a rectangular garden
EDINBURGH

This garden with long straight boundaries needed a path to give access from the house to the garage at the far end of the plot. As the back of the house faces almost due south, an area of paving, sixteen feet deep, is planned outside the french doors. This allows room for a rose garden, and a seat, with a view across the garden to a small conifer or ornament, recessed in a rose border. This enclosed garden treatment near the house helps to break up the length of the plot.

The paving gives access to a small shed and then continues as a curved path, flanking a shrub border and an area for salads, to lead through a vegetable garden and on to a gate through a woven fence, to the drive and garage.

A shrub border gives added privacy on the south-east boundary, but is curved out to allow for a bold planting of flowers. This flower border combines with the gentle curve of the paved path to give a pleasant outline to the lawn, disguising the formal boundaries of the site. A small flowering tree on the lawn adds to the informality and screens out the side of the garage from the house windows.

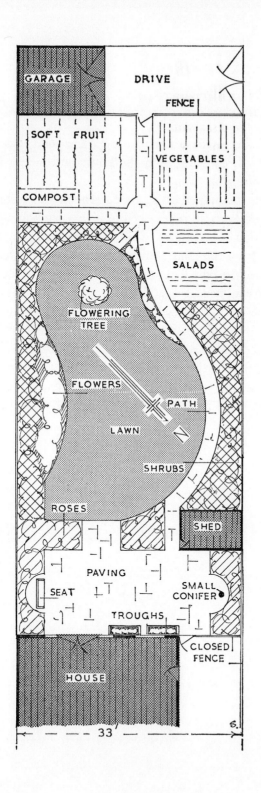

GARAGE

DRIVE

FENCE

SOFT FRUIT

VEGETABLES

COMPOST

SALADS

FLOWERING
TREE

FLOWERS

PATH

LAWN

SHRUBS

ROSES

SHED

PAVING

SEAT

SMALL
CONIFER

TROUGHS

CLOSED
FENCE

HOUSE

33

S.

Garage in a rectangular back garden
MELTON MOWBRAY, LEICESTERSHIRE

This site has the disadvantage of the garage being placed well inside the back garden, on view from the house and taking away much of the width of the plot.

The back of the house gets all the afternoon and evening sun, so the existing line of concrete is enlarged to give a semi-circular paved area, with rose or flower beds, backed by climbers, screening the side of the garage. Seen from the house, this gives the effect of a formal colourful rose garden, extending to the informal lawn with its curved shrub borders and island bed for low shrubs.

Use is made of the full width of the garden beyond the garage to have a paved recess for a seat, set facing south and framed by flower borders. Closed fencing on this north boundary gives an unexpected secluded area, reached by stepping stones from the formal rose garden.

A path continues, to the west, to give access to the shed and vegetable garden, and a small flowering tree in the south-west corner is effective as seen from the seat and from the house.

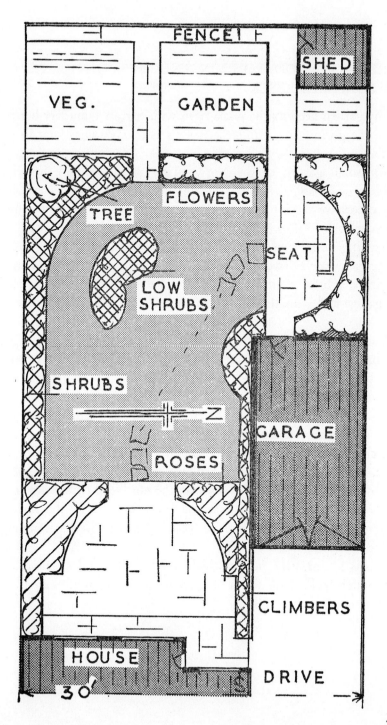

Tiny gardens
UPPER NORWOOD, LONDON AND
HESTON, MIDDLESEX

A tiny garden need not be just a lawn with narrow boundary borders. It can be given a lot of interest as long as everything is kept in proportion.

The small garden of the Norwood terrace house had the added problem of linking the house with the detached garage. It was solved in a decorative fashion by extending the paving near the house into a deep curve.

Stepping stones curve from the paving, across the tiny lawn, to lead to the garage and drive. The boundary borders curve to give room for varying depths of planting. A small tree helps to screen out the side of the garage and a small specimen shrub could be added on the lawn.

A small garden with high walls may be deeply shaded and damp, or else baked dry by constant sunshine, according to its aspect. In either case it is sometimes worth relying on a combination of paving materials to give contrast.

The walled garden at Heston, viewed from a study window, has been made decorative without the use of grass.

A circular crazy-paved path surrounding rose beds has a brick centre piece, with a small ornament set on cobbles. Borders for climbers, shrubs and flowers soften the walls. In the north-east corner is a raised recess with room for a seat, set on brick paving. In the opposite corners, other recesses allow room for two small conifers, set amongst cobbles.

This is a trim, neat garden which could be kept full of colour, but has enough basic construction to make it interesting at all seasons.

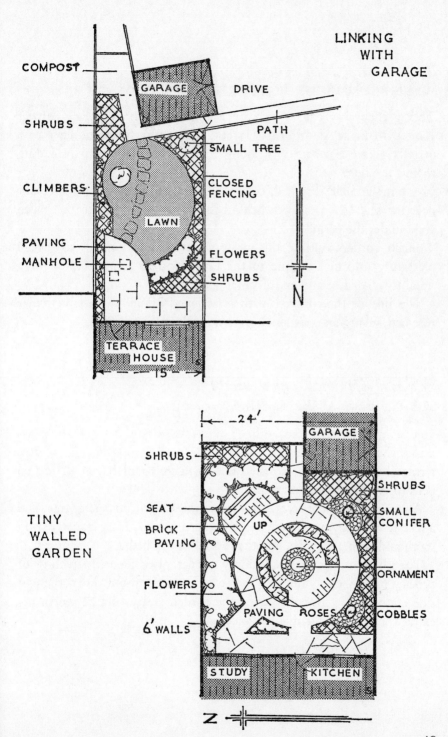

LINKING
WITH
GARAGE

COMPOST

GARAGE   DRIVE

SHRUBS

PATH

SMALL TREE

CLIMBERS

CLOSED
FENCING

LAWN

PAVING

FLOWERS

MANHOLE

SHRUBS

N

TERRACE
HOUSE

15

24'

GARAGE

SHRUBS

TINY
WALLED
GARDEN

SEAT

UP

SHRUBS

SMALL
CONIFER

BRICK
PAVING

FLOWERS

ORNAMENT

6' WALLS

PAVING   ROSES

COBBLES

STUDY   KITCHEN

Z

Square site with concrete path
WEST BROMWICH, STAFFORDSHIRE

This garden was cut in two by a concrete path. The new owner wanted to make an informal layout. The path now terminates in a pergola giving privacy right along the end boundary and providing room for a seat.

A semi-circular rose bed, cut in half by the old path, gives colour near the seat. A grass walk behind the roses links up with the paved walk under the pergola.

Shrub borders outline this grass walk and are curved, to give a pleasantly informal outline to the lawn, and to form recesses for a small shrub or tree and an informal pool.

The line of the concrete path is softened by another semi-circular rose bed, giving an additional grass walk round the garden.

Square site with cross views
SOLIHULL, WARWICKSHIRE

One way to disguise the outlines of a square plot is to create views across the garden. The narrow concrete path across the rear of this terrace house has been widened out to make room for small formal beds for vivid seasonal planting.

A curved shrub border gives a recess for a small flowering tree, and a recess, with paving, in the north corner gives room for a seat, facing south and with a view back to the formal flower beds.

The shape of the east boundary border gives an extra feeling of privacy to the seat, while a glimpse of lawn extension down the east side of the house gives length to the garden and would be worth the extra work needed for maintenance.

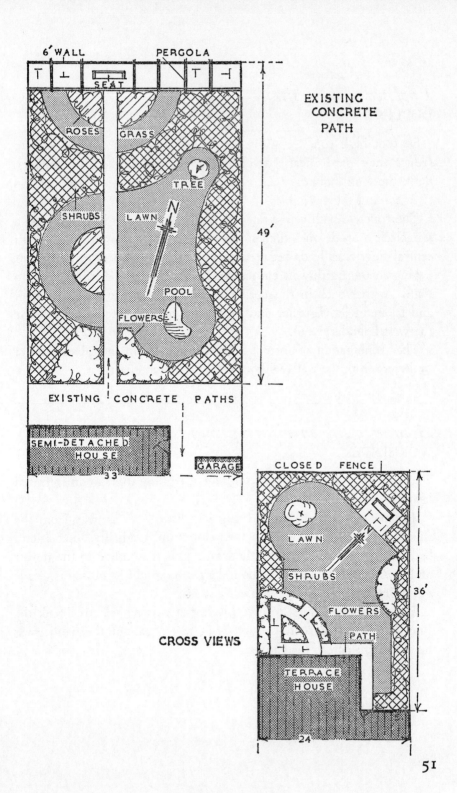

6' WALL   PERGOLA

SEAT

EXISTING
CONCRETE
PATH

ROSES   GRASS

TREE

SHRUBS   LAWN

N

POOL

FLOWERS

49'

EXISTING CONCRETE PATHS

SEMI-DETACHED
HOUSE

33

GARAGE

CLOSED FENCE

LAWN

SHRUBS

FLOWERS

PATH

36'

CROSS VIEWS

TERRACE
HOUSE

24

51

Enclosed square site
DUBLIN

Six-foot high concrete walls dominate this garden, and to help to reduce their hard effect, curved flower borders, backed by climbers, flank the south boundary and turn across the garden as shrub borders to screen out the vegetables.

The concrete path across the rear of the house is widened out into a semicircle outside the kitchen door. From here, a grass path with central flagstones leads between shrub and rose borders to a circle of paving in the north-west corner. Use is made of the existing walls to build up rockwork in this corner as a background to a circular pool and fountain jet. Espalier and bush fruit help to disguise and clothe the west boundary wall.

The combination of formal and informal treatments gives interest to detract from the walls without creating a fussy effect.

A square site on rising ground
WORCESTER

The land rises up away from the house, lending itself to an informal layout.

The patio is curved out to bring it a little further away from the shade of the house. The lawn then slopes up, gradually, to an island bed for roses or shrubs. Together with a curved outline to the flower and shrub border on the east boundary, this would form a grass glade effect, leading to a seat recess, facing south.

Three specimen trees, to give interest at varying seasons, break the line of the west corner. Cordon fruit to the east of the patio gives height to this part of the garden.

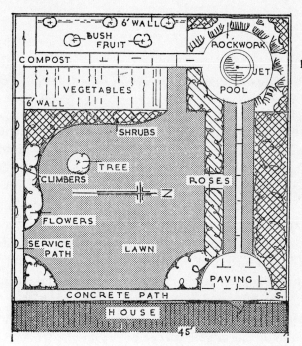

ENCLOSED SITE

In the plan (labels):
6' WALL
BUSH FRUIT
COMPOST
VEGETABLES
6' WALL
SHRUBS
ROCKWORK
JET
POOL
TREE
CLIMBERS
ROSES
FLOWERS
SERVICE PATH
LAWN
PAVING
CONCRETE PATH
HOUSE
45'
S.

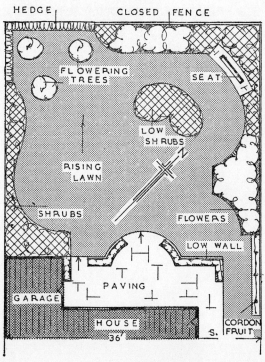

ON RISING GROUND

In the plan (labels):
HEDGE
CLOSED FENCE
FLOWERING TREES
SEAT
LOW SHRUBS
RISING LAWN
SHRUBS
FLOWERS
LOW WALL
PAVING
GARAGE
HOUSE
CORDON FRUIT
36'
S.

53

Odd-shaped plot
WOLVERHAMPTON, STAFFORDSHIRE

This site combines the problems of the square garden with a long, narrow plot. Near the house, a central lawn is surrounded by concrete paths, flanked by wide boundary flower borders, and by cutting into the very unwieldy border on the west boundary, there is room for a paved area and a seat. Shrub planting in the remaining part of the border gives privacy and shelter to the seat, and still allows room for flower planting in front of the shrubs.

A semi-circle of paving in the border opposite the seat allows room for an ornament such as a bird bath. Without disturbing the existing concrete paths the whole garden is made more interesting and easier to manage.

The rest of the site extends as a long, narrow section, with a concrete path continuing right to the north boundary.

To give a little more informality to the garden, the first part of this path is broken to form stepping stones through a lawn, planted with naturalised bulbs and screened on the north and east sides by cordon fruit trees. Beyond this section the existing path makes for easy maintenance of the vegetable garden and gives access to the shed and compost area.

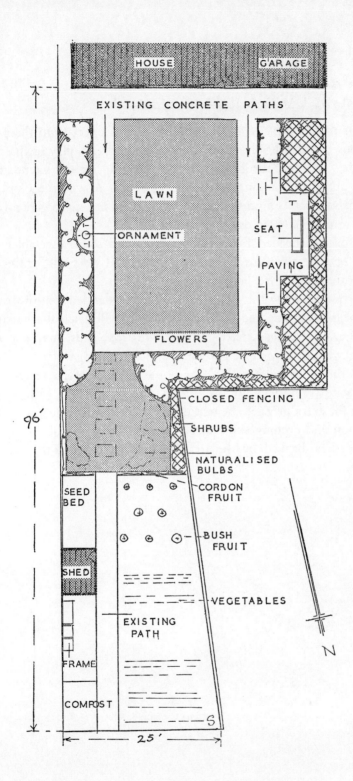

HOUSE   GARAGE

EXISTING CONCRETE PATHS

LAWN

ORNAMENT

SEAT

PAVING

FLOWERS

CLOSED FENCING

SHRUBS

NATURALISED BULBS

CORDON FRUIT

BUSH FRUIT

SEED BED

SHED

VEGETABLES

EXISTING PATH

FRAME

COMPOST

96'

25'

N

S

Space at the side
CHORLEY, LANCASHIRE

On this plot, the far boundary is only thirty-six feet from the rear of the house, so this has been left clear as a children's play lawn, except for a few flowers, shrubs and conifer hedging on the boundaries to screen out large buildings in the background. A workshop and shed are tucked away behind the garage, with extra paving to give access to them from the kitchen door.

As space is needed for a clothes drier and some vegetables there would be little room for a pleasure garden, if it were not for the space at the south side of the house.

The paving along the rear of the house is extended southwards into a circle to accommodate the drier, where it will catch the maximum sunshine. The paved circle, outlined with rose beds, makes a useful link between the vegetable garden and the pleasure garden.

A path to the south side of the house leads to a seat recess. Here, set amongst flowers and backed by screen walling, with a shrub border for extra privacy, the seat is in a quiet corner which gets all the afternoon and evening sun and has a view across a small lawn to the rose borders, backed by the trellis which screens out the vegetable garden.

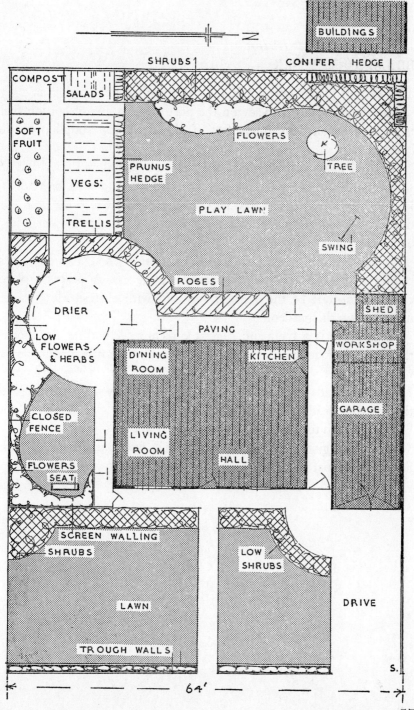

BUILDINGS

SHRUBS   CONIFER HEDGE

COMPOST

SALADS

SOFT
FRUIT

VEGS:

TRELLIS

PRUNUS
HEDGE

FLOWERS

TREE

PLAY LAWN

SWING

ROSES

DRIER

LOW
FLOWERS
& HERBS

PAVING

SHED

WORKSHOP

DINING
ROOM

KITCHEN

CLOSED
FENCE

LIVING
ROOM

HALL

GARAGE

FLOWERS

SEAT

SCREEN WALLING

SHRUBS

LOW
SHRUBS

LAWN

DRIVE

TROUGH WALLS

S.

64'

57

A long, thin garden
BILLERICAY, ESSEX

This extremely narrow plot has a well-trimmed field hedge along its south boundary. For privacy on the north side, a line of cordon fruit is planted beyond the thirty feet of closed fencing supplied by the builders.

A paved patio with sloping bank, and an uncluttered lawn for the small family to enjoy, is planned for the sun-trap area beyond the kitchen window. Curved rose borders close this lawn to the east, cutting off the length of the plot and forming a background for a bird bath, set amongst flowers.

Privacy is given to the next section by a conifer hedge on two sides, behind a shrub border with a paved seat recess. A peaceful place, catching the last of the western sun and with a fresh view across, instead of up the garden.

Beyond this is a fruit and vegetable section. A path at the foot of the established hedge uses up land which would not be profitable for vegetables, and makes for easy maintenance of both hedge and crops.

The path leads on past an old oak and a play lawn to give access to the footpath leading to a nearby park. This entrance is paved, and hedging is used to screen out the compost heap.

The design gives an unobtrusive dry walk from kitchen to footpath, linking the separate gardens which disguise the length of the plot.

A LONG THIN GARDEN

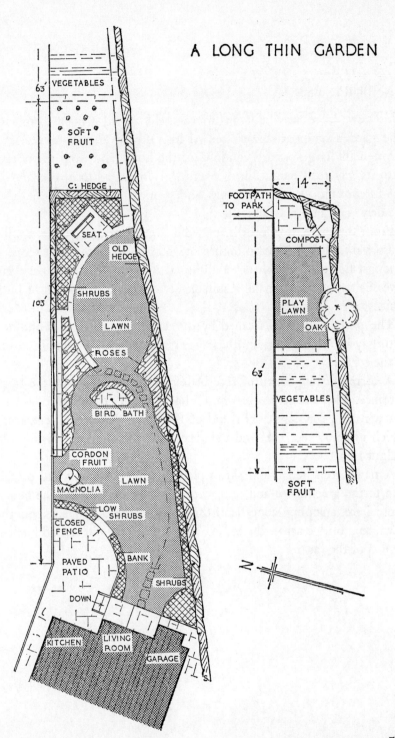

VEGETABLES

63'

SOFT
FRUIT

C: HEDGE

SEAT

OLD
HEDGE

SHRUBS

103'

LAWN

ROSES

BIRD BATH

CORDON
FRUIT

LAWN

MAGNOLIA

LOW
SHRUBS

CLOSED
FENCE

BANK

PAVED
PATIO

SHRUBS

DOWN

KITCHEN

LIVING
ROOM

GARAGE

S

FOOTPATH
TO PARK

14'

COMPOST

PLAY
LAWN

OAK

63'

VEGETABLES

SOFT
FRUIT

N

The larger garden
DANBURY, ESSEX

This new house was built on a level field amongst open farmland. The garden boundaries were settled by studying the extensive views through the large picture windows of the house and from the terrace with its gay rock bank. Shrub planting is arranged to give colour in the foreground of the main view and grouped towards the south, at the drive entrance, to frame the view.

From the drive, northwards, past the front door and garage, a wide grass walk flanked by twin herbaceous borders leads to a seat recessed amongst flowers. New shrubs and the existing old hedge and parkland give shelter here and make a suitable setting for a plantation of bush fruit.

The paved courtyard formed by the angle of the house is outlined with gay bedding plants and has a central pool with a fountain figure in the corner.

A formal arrangement of rose beds gives colour opposite the front entrance. The rose screen forming a background also helps to obscure the wire run for dogs at the end of the drive. A circular seat, from which to enjoy the roses and the view, is built round an existing old walnut tree.

A new beech hedge and shrub planting give screening and protection to the greenhouse and utility areas on the west side of the house. From here, stepping stones lead through the beech hedge, across the lawn, to a bridge across the old moat and on to the old walled kitchen garden of the farm.

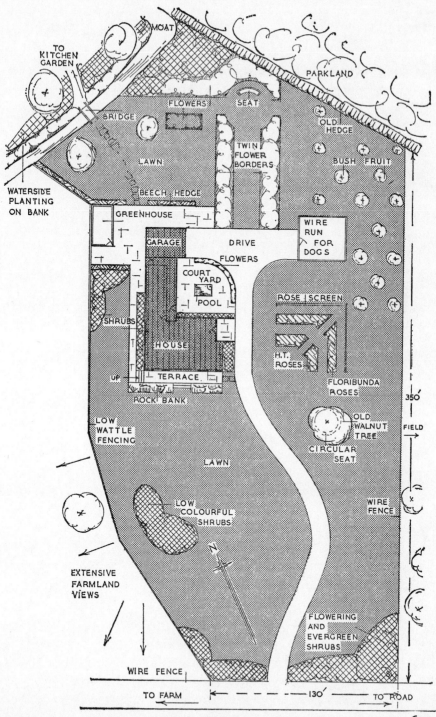

TO
KITCHEN
GARDEN

MOAT

PARKLAND

BRIDGE

FLOWERS

SEAT

OLD
HEDGE

LAWN

TWIN
FLOWER
BORDERS

BUSH FRUIT

WATERSIDE
PLANTING
ON BANK

BEECH HEDGE

GREENHOUSE

GARAGE

DRIVE

WIRE
RUN
FOR
DOGS

FLOWERS

COURT
YARD

POOL

ROSE SCREEN

SHRUBS

HOUSE

H.T.
ROSES

TERRACE

ROCK BANK

FLORIBUNDA
ROSES

UP

LOW
WATTLE
FENCING

OLD
WALNUT
TREE

CIRCULAR
SEAT

350'

FIELD

LAWN

LOW
COLOURFUL
SHRUBS

N

WIRE
FENCE

EXTENSIVE
FARMLAND
VIEWS

FLOWERING
AND
EVERGREEN
SHRUBS

WIRE FENCE

TO FARM

130'

TO ROAD

4 A setting for the house

The sort of house you live in will tend to dictate the design of your garden. With a terrace house, you cannot hope to find room for all the features you can achieve in the wider garden of a detached house. Yet, even in the smallest garden it is possible, with thoughtful planning and wise planting, to create some element of surprise; something which cannot be seen at a glance from the house windows; a trick of design which tempts you out into the garden to explore.

With enclosed town gardens this can be achieved quickly by making use of the many modern aids now available, such as screen walling, a sudden splash of coloured paving, or a mature container shrub in a strategic position.

For the garden of the semi-detached house, privacy is usually the main need. Closed fencing may be essential near the house but fencing all round the garden can be very dull and cuts out a good deal of air and sunlight. Privacy can be achieved by planting cordon fruit on a boundary or quick-growing hedge plants such as conifers, (*Cupressocyparis leylandii*) or an evergreen cotoneaster (*C. lactea*). A prickly hedge such as berberis or shrub roses might be desirable but will eventually take three to four feet off the width of the garden. In that space, a mixed planting of flowering shrubs could give greater interest over a long period of the year.

The skilful placing of an island shrub bed can give privacy just where it is needed, avoiding the dullness of a straight boundary hedge.

With a bungalow garden, privacy is probably more important near the building than on the boundaries. A thoughtful arrangement of paths and planting can achieve this, combined with the ample access required.

A typical cottage garden contains a profusion of planting allowed to seed and grow at will. A little extra care in aligning paths on the angles of the building and ensuring they are wide enough for easy walking, will help to make the garden manageable and attractive throughout the winter.

With a house of architectural interest this link between house and garden should be emphasised. Any constructional material used in the garden should harmonise with the house in colour and texture.

A cottage with a shallow garden
GODALMING, SURREY

There is plenty of width to this garden, but the south boundary is only thirty-two feet away from the rear of the cottage.

A small area of paving between rose borders, outside the living-room door, leads straight on to the lawn. Two island beds are planned to give a greater feeling of depth to the garden by providing grass walks between them and the south boundary shrub border.

The illusion of depth is increased by curved borders turning towards a seat in the south-east corner, set in the shade of an existing tree.

Use is made of the space behind the garage to create a paved, formal flower garden with raised beds, giving extra height and so reducing some of the width of the garden in relation to its shallowness. An arch between the flower beds adds to this effect, and screens out the utility area with its greenhouse, frames, shed and compost area.

This arrangement of raised beds and greenhouse, surrounded by level paving, close to the kitchen door, would provide a section of the garden which could be enjoyed and maintained by an elderly or handicapped person.

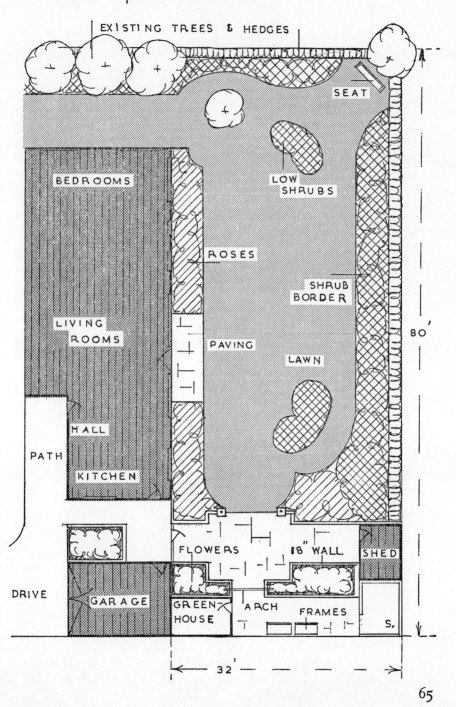

N

EXISTING TREES & HEDGES

SEAT

LOW SHRUBS

BEDROOMS

ROSES

SHRUB BORDER

LIVING ROOMS

PAVING

LAWN

80'

HALL

PATH

KITCHEN

FLOWERS

18" WALL

SHED

DRIVE

GARAGE

GREEN HOUSE

ARCH

FRAMES

S.

32'

An L-shaped house
WICKFORD, ESSEX

The interesting shape of this house allows room for plenty of paving outside the kitchen and living room doors, making an excellent play area for small children. A sand pit could be included here, if desired and developed as a pool in later years.

The more secluded part of the garden in the north corner allows room for a circle of paving or grass, with a seat facing south. Interest could be added to this level site by outlining this circle with low dry walling. Front crevices planted with alpines would soften the general effect and add easily maintained colour to this part of the garden.

The path leading to the seat turns to give unobtrusive access to the compost area.

The curved south boundary border is planted with shrubs and gives an interesting shape to the lawn, and screens the neighbouring house. This layout is decorative while allowing plenty of room for children to play without doing much damage.

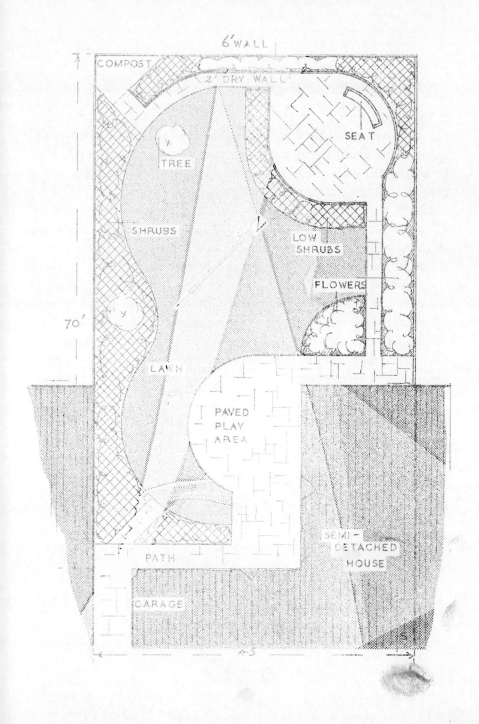

6' WALL

COMPOST

2' DRY WALL

SEAT

TREE

SHRUBS

LOW
SHRUBS

FLOWERS

70'

LAWN

PAVED
PLAY
AREA

SEMI-
DETACHED
HOUSE

PATH

GARAGE

A bungalow garden
THATCHAM, BERKSHIRE

A little space to spare on the south side of this bungalow allows room for an extensive paved area, linking the doors from the kitchen and living-room. From the double doors, two breaks in the flower border encircling the paving lead to the main lawn and, by stepping stones, give access to the rear of the distant garage.

The borders defining the paving outside the kitchen door are raised a few inches, to make for easier management of the rose planting and clean maintenance of the paved area.

Shrubs are planted to give greater privacy to the south roadside boundary on this corner site. Screen block walling, and a gate level with the east front of the bungalow, make for privacy from the front garden.

This layout would give a garden very suitable for management by a retired couple, or business people with little time to spare for gardening.

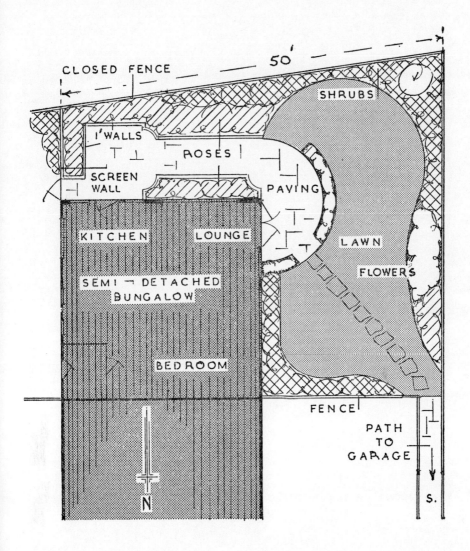

CLOSED FENCE — — 50' — — —

SHRUBS

1' WALLS

ROSES

SCREEN WALL

PAVING

KITCHEN LOUNGE

LAWN

SEMI-DETACHED BUNGALOW

FLOWERS

BEDROOM

FENCE

N

PATH TO GARAGE

S.

Detached house with a picture window
MEOPHAM, KENT

A large picture window overlooking a garden calls for variety in the layout to save the view from being monotonous. Paving, outside the south-east facing window, is outlined with rose borders, giving the feeling of a small, intimate garden near the house.

Privacy is given to the window by climbers on the north boundary, and these form a background for an island bed of perennials, thus creating the view of a grass walk, leading to a seat recessed in the east corner. A small ornament or bird bath might be included here, if desired. From the seat there is a fresh view westwards across the garden, completely different from the one so familiar from the picture window.

The shrub border on the west boundary is shaped to form a small circular lawn near the kitchen door. An extra depth of border allows for flower planting, before curving round behind an island bed for low growing shrubs. This gives colour on a diagonal view as seen from the picture window, and screens out the compost area.

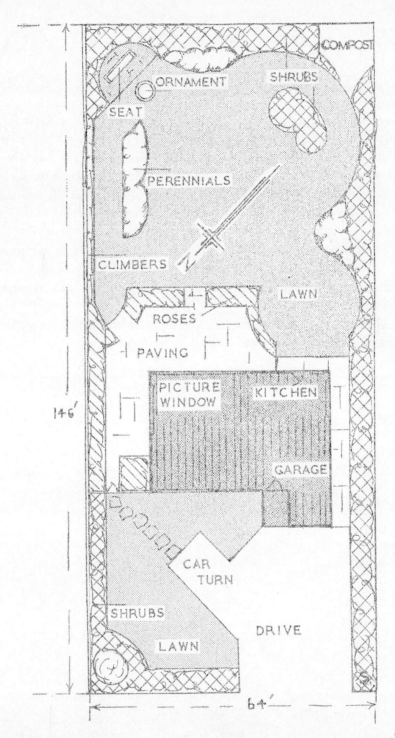

COMPOST

ORNAMENT

SHRUBS

SEAT

PERENNIALS

CLIMBERS

LAWN

ROSES

PAVING

PICTURE
WINDOW

KITCHEN

GARAGE

CAR
TURN

SHRUBS

DRIVE

LAWN

146'

64'

A detached house
BRAMHOPE, LEEDS

There is just space at the east side of this house to allow room for a grass verge flanking the side path and backed by a well-established old boundary hedge. This would be restful as seen from the house windows, and would set off the building as seen from the main road.

Curved flower and rose beds in the front garden add the necessary splash of colour. Extra paving gives a dignified approach to the front door.

The lawn of the small back garden is shaped to give a maximum of width outside the living-room doors and then narrows down to a secluded area, surrounded by shrubs, screening out the small vegetable and soft fruit areas.

The seat set on paving is placed in the sunniest part of the garden, backed by the old hedge and flanked by flowers.

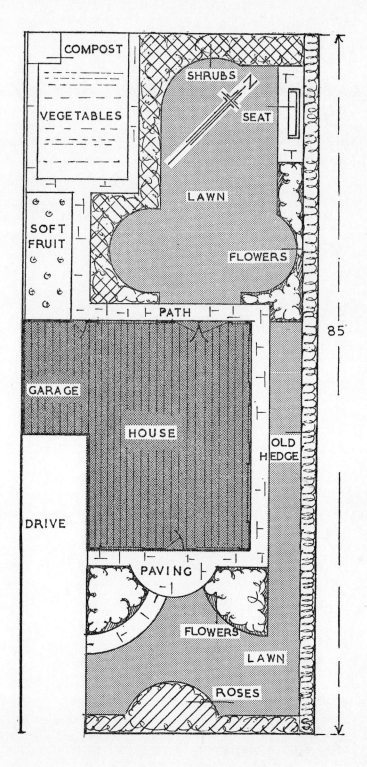

COMPOST

VEGETABLES

SHRUBS

SEAT

SOFT
FRUIT

LAWN

FLOWERS

85'

PATH

GARAGE

HOUSE

OLD
HEDGE

DRIVE

PAVING

FLOWERS

LAWN

ROSES

A semi-detached house
EDINBURGH

Space was needed for vegetables, and the most unobtrusive place seemed to be beyond the kitchen. To compensate for the dull outlook to the north, the west-facing window of the kitchen has a pleasant view of a sweeping lawn, set off by an island shrub bed and small flowering trees.

Extra paving outside the kitchen door, together with curved borders screening the vegetable garden from the main lawn, enhances the informality of this small, squarish garden.

An ample paved recess allows room for a seat set facing south and helps to cut into the depth of the corner shrub border, and so make for easier maintenance.

The front garden is planted as a rose garden, balanced on the lines of the existing path to the front door and screening the drive as seen from the living-room windows.

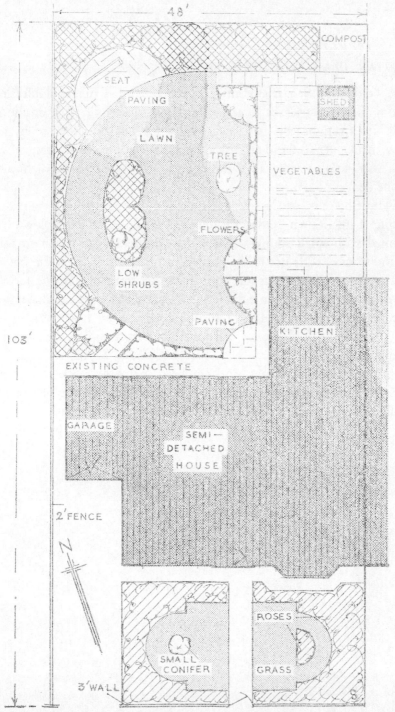

48'

COMPOST

SEAT

PAVING

LAWN

SHED

TREE

VEGETABLES

FLOWERS

LOW
SHRUBS

103'

PAVING

KITCHEN

EXISTING CONCRETE

GARAGE

SEMI—
DETACHED
HOUSE

2'FENCE

N

ROSES

SMALL
CONIFER

GRASS

3'WALL

A Georgian-style house
LUTON, BEDFORDSHIRE

The bold, dignified layout of this walled garden makes a pleasing setting for the clear-cut lines of the house. From the side entrance, with its wrought-iron gateway, paving extends to allow room for movement outside the door of the house. A path leads, in front of an oval pool, to give access to a grass terrace, which forms the main part of the design.

Flower borders, on the south boundary and under the large window, outline a small lawn, setting off the pool which is flanked by low piers planted with small conifers. A fountain jet, set in the retaining wall of the terrace, adds life to the garden picture as seen from the house.

The slight variation in levels given by the formation of the terrace helps to detract from the boundary walls, and ensures that the seating here catches the maximum of sunshine. A narrow flower bed gives colour in front of the seats, and forms a background to the fountain and pool.

A few flowering shrubs, and climbers, including some evergreen, are grouped in the boundary flower borders to break the line of the walls and give shape to the garden during the winter months.

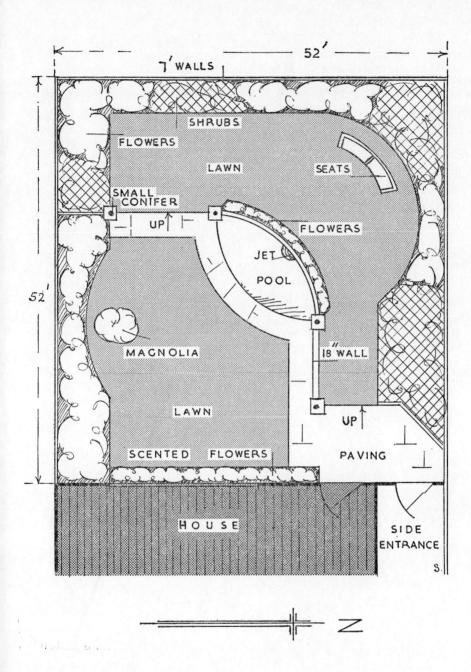

52'

7' WALLS

SHRUBS

FLOWERS

LAWN

SEATS

SMALL
CONIFER

UP

FLOWERS

JET

POOL

52'

MAGNOLIA

18" WALL

LAWN

UP

SCENTED   FLOWERS

PAVING

HOUSE

SIDE
ENTRANCE

S.

N

Three front gardens
WOODFORD, ESSEX; BURY, LANCASHIRE;
AND LEICESTER

In the Woodford plan, a modernised front garden dropping below the bay window of the house makes use of stonework and varied shrub planting to give a neat, permanent, labour-saving layout. This replaces a time-consuming arrangement of overgrown rock banks.

From the short drive to the garage, curved retaining walls allow extra room for car passengers to alight. A paved path curves up between twelve-inch high walls, by wide gradual steps, to the front porch.

The flanking borders are planted with heaths in variety. Evergreen and deciduous azaleas are planted on the north side behind an eighteen-inch wall. The border is still well below the damp course of the bay window. The two existing small conifers are retained as an asset to the design.

A separate pedestrian entrance leads by gentle steps to the front door and the old front wall is planted with prostrate shrubs such as junipers and cotoneasters. Neat shrub planting in a narrow trough bed on the north boundary gives a little necessary privacy here.

The front garden at Bury, facing north-east, is overlooked by a picture window, so the layout is planned to give a complete garden scene. Curved shrub borders are outlined by cobbles and a cobbled recess makes a setting for a small flowering tree. Seasonal flowers, to give vivid colour, are introduced in a circular central flower bed and in an L-shaped bed near the front porch.

The lawn has a pleasing outline and is open to the drive and the path round to the side entrance.

An open plan front garden in Leicester is given a little privacy by adapting a necessary retaining wall to allow for trough planting on the east boundary, ending in some shrub planting at the front roadside.

From a square of paving by the front door, stepping stones lead across the lawn to the drive entrance to save all visitors coming past the living-room window. Low shrub planting softens the paving outline. A small tree and specimen shrub are set on the lawn, where they will give further privacy to the house.

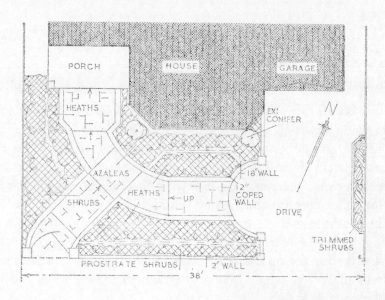

PORCH

HOUSE

GARAGE

HEATHS

EX!
CONIFER

N

AZALEAS

18" WALL

HEATHS

UP

12"
COPED
WALL

SHRUBS

DRIVE

TRIMMED
SHRUBS

PROSTRATE SHRUBS 2' WALL

38'

THREE
FRONT
GARDENS

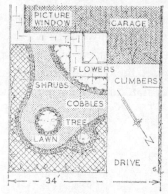

PICTURE
WINDOW

GARAGE

FLOWERS

CLIMBERS

SHRUBS

COBBLES

TREE

N

LAWN

DRIVE

34'

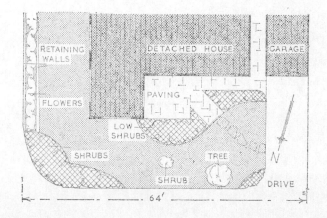

RETAINING
WALLS

DETACHED HOUSE

GARAGE

PAVING

FLOWERS

LOW
SHRUBS

SHRUBS

TREE

N

SHRUB

DRIVE

64'

An end terrace house
CHELMSFORD, ESSEX

Use has been made of every corner of this small garden to provide for the varying needs of a growing family. The side entrance gate was blocked to give a secluded flower garden with a paved seat recess and a central circle of grass. Set slightly below the rest of the garden and entered between the piers of a low wall, this makes a restful garden catching the afternoon and evening sunshine.

The existing concrete outside the back door now leads down to paving under the existing small flowering trees, making an ideal courtyard effect for meals out of doors. A low wall and shrubs screen it from the drive, which is now the family's main entrance to the garden.

An open lawn for play has the interest of an informal pool and rockwork in the awkward north-east corner.

The front garden is kept purely decorative, with ample paving setting off the pleasant old house and a colourful rock bank backed by roses flanking the corner of the roadway.

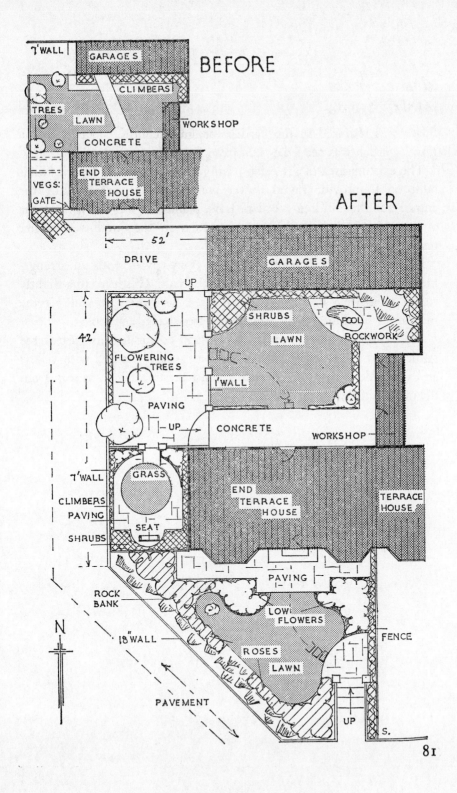

BEFORE

7' WALL

GARAGES

CLIMBERS

TREES

LAWN

WORKSHOP

CONCRETE

END
TERRACE
HOUSE

VEGS:

GATE

AFTER

52'

DRIVE

GARAGES

UP

42'

SHRUBS

LAWN

POOL

ROCKWORK

FLOWERING
TREES

PAVING

1' WALL

UP

CONCRETE

WORKSHOP

7' WALL

GRASS

END
TERRACE
HOUSE

TERRACE
HOUSE

CLIMBERS

PAVING

SEAT

SHRUBS

PAVING

ROCK
BANK

LOW
FLOWERS

N

18" WALL

ROSES

LAWN

FENCE

UP

S.

PAVEMENT

A town house
LONDON, W.14.

Space was required in the garden for small children to play, but a flower garden was needed as seen from the house.

The existing area of grey slab paving is used as a basis for low walls built up to provide raised flower borders, wtih piers flanking the entrance to the children's section. Low, planted flower bowls mark the outline of the slabs, which are repeated in the south-west corner reserved for the children's swing.

For contrast, the remaining area is crazy-paved, with an arrangement of green coloured slabs suggesting a path. This leads to a slightly raised semi-circle of paving, with a seat set where it will get the maximum sunshine in this walled and tree-shaded garden.

Wall climbers and more low bowls add colour to this part of the garden, and a raised bed against the west wall is planted with yellow and white flowers, to be effective against the tree shade, as seen from the main window of the house.

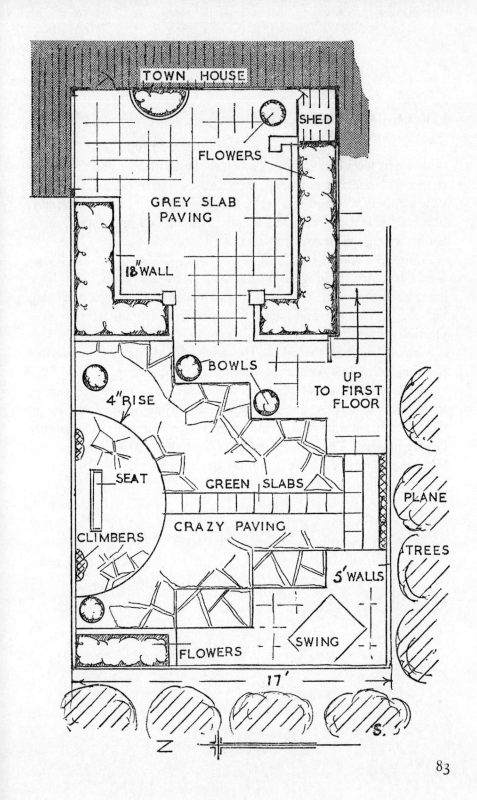

TOWN HOUSE

SHED

FLOWERS

GREY SLAB
PAVING

18" WALL

BOWLS

UP
TO FIRST
FLOOR

4" RISE

SEAT

GREEN SLABS

PLANE

CLIMBERS

CRAZY PAVING

TREES

5' WALLS

SWING

FLOWERS

17'

N

S.

83

A split-level house
LITTLE BADDOW, ESSEX

A drive through an apple orchard leads to the farm office and garages of this split level house. Steps lead up to the front door and the living-rooms. A corner terrace, some eight feet above the main lawn, has a view across to a curved rose walk, backed by a newly planted spinney. Shrubs clothe the terrace walls, and an island bed and curved shrub border screen out the soft fruit area.

From the kitchen door, facing east, paving gives access to the house-wife's secluded little garden, screened from the main lawn by a lavender hedge. A few flowers, a seat and a herb border screening out the greenhouse and salad area, combine to make this a very practical yet restful corner of the garden.

A small brook at the side of the drive is made gay with waterside planting, combined with a planting of spring flowering shrubs.

Shrubs to the west of the drive are chosen for summer flowering, to follow the display of apple blossom. To the west of the lawn, shrubs with autumn foliage and berries take over from the summer display of roses. The shrub plantings frame views of the orchard, and bring the charm of the trees into the garden picture.

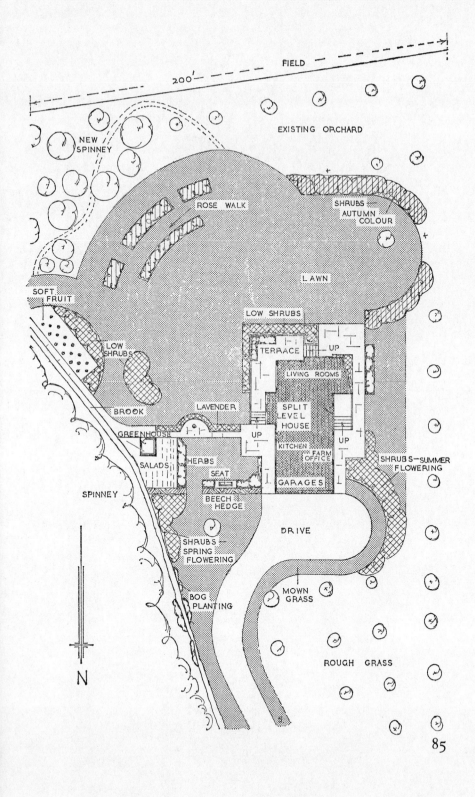

FIELD

200'

EXISTING ORCHARD

NEW
SPINNEY

ROSE WALK

SHRUBS—
AUTUMN
COLOUR

LAWN

SOFT
FRUIT

LOW SHRUBS

LOW
SHRUBS

TERRACE

UP

LIVING ROOMS

BROOK

LAVENDER

SPLIT
LEVEL
HOUSE

GREENHOUSE

UP

KITCHEN

UP

SALADS

HERBS

SEAT

FARM
OFFICE

SHRUBS—SUMMER
FLOWERING

SPINNEY

BEECH
HEDGE

GARAGES

DRIVE

N

SHRUBS—
SPRING
FLOWERING

BOG
PLANTING

MOWN
GRASS

ROUGH GRASS

85

5 Special problems

Every garden site has individual problems. No two are exactly alike, and no two owners have exactly the same tastes and requirements. It is this possibility of expressing one's own personality that gives the thrill to garden making. It is a chance to create something unique. The more difficulties the site presents, the greater the challenge.

Even a garden with wide views across open countryside needs careful planning to frame the view in the garden picture, otherwise most of the interest of the garden is lost.

A site with surrounding buildings enclosing it, especially when they are near enough to cast deep shade, calls for careful arrangement of plant material, so that the buildings can be made to enhance, rather than spoil the garden background.

Existing trees can often help to dictate the design of the garden and give it an established look straight away but overgrown old gardens raise special planning problems. The great temptation is to clear the site ruthlessly but if possible it is worth waiting a year round before making drastic changes. Undergrowth may conceal interesting plants or bulbs, and old trees may prove to give a very welcome screen during the winter months.

Apart from natural features, many gardens have to contend with man-made obstacles like concrete paths and manhole covers. Wise planning and planting can help to make these less obvious.

Strong winds often eddy round houses which are built close together. Immediate protection with woven or wattle fencing may be advisable while screen planting is getting established for a long-term display.

Whatever your site contains, try and make use of it to give individuality to your garden. Work with these features, rather than fight against them.

Existing manholes
SEDGLEY, STAFFORDSHIRE

Manhole covers can be a real eyesore, especially in a new, bare plot. But with forethought they can be incorporated into the layout of the garden and may even suggest the design.

On this site they are very obtrusive, so they are used to form the central feature of a formal rose garden. A lightweight sundial or bird bath placed on the covers is surrounded by a bed of shallow-rooting alpines or small miniature roses. The arrangement of the larger rose borders gives an intimate, secluded feeling from the kitchen door and the large window of the living-room. A small specimen conifer and a permanent seat add to the restful effect.

Beyond this, the garden is treated informally, with curved boundary shrub borders disguising the awkward shape of the plot. A flowering tree and an island bed for perennials give extra colour, as seen from the house.

With manholes sited near the house, the level of paving or concrete can sometimes be adjusted to include them. Another alternative is to plant a prostrate shrub such as a cotoneaster or juniper to fall over them. Lightweight containers are available which can be placed safely on the manhole cover and planted either with permanent low-growing shrubs or a seasonal display of bulbs followed by bedding plants.

EXISTING MANHOLES

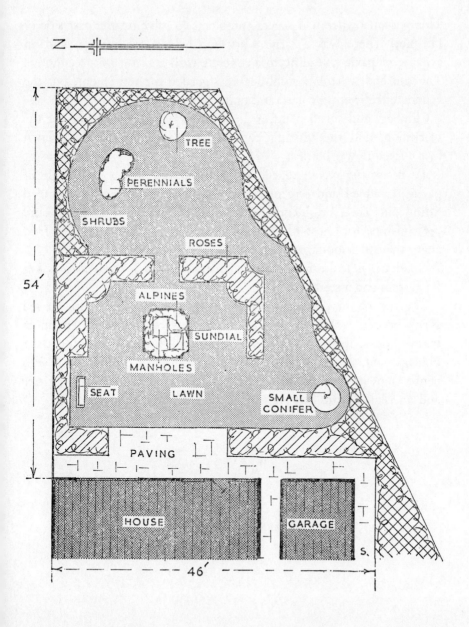

Inherited concrete
DUMFRIES

This garden owner had several problems to solve on the east side of his plot. There was a large workshop behind the garage, and an expanse of paving, leading to a concrete path and a large greenhouse. The site had several possibilities as a garden for retirement, but the general effect was very hard and uninviting.

Climbers and shrub planting help to disguise the hard lines of the workshop, and the existing path is screened from the main lawn by a curved flower border.

To break the rectangular lines of the paved area a semi-circle of paving is added and screened round with shrubs to give a secluded sitting out place, brightened with bowls of flowers. The area would get sunshine for most of the day. Privacy is given by cordon fruit along the east boundary.

Good use is to be made of the greenhouse, so a small area is left for frames and a seed bed.

The rest of the garden is informal and labour-saving, with curved shrub borders, interspersed with large flower groupings. An unobtrusive line of flagstones between shrubs and flowers makes for easier management. A slight fall in the lawn allows for a grass bank with gentle steps leading down to a lower lawn, in which a flowering tree and an island shrub bed add to the general relaxing effect.

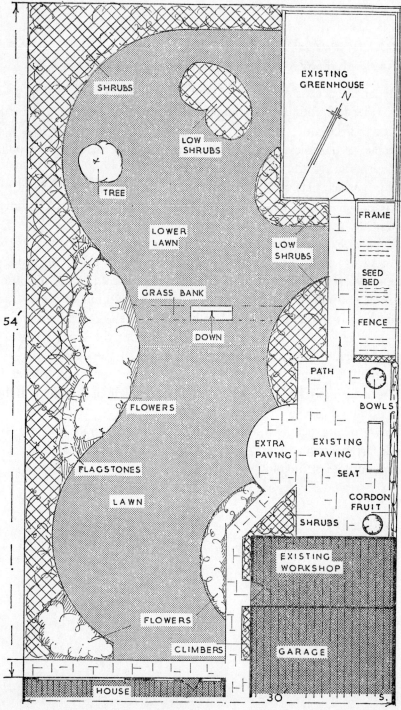

SHRUBS

LOW SHRUBS

EXISTING GREENHOUSE

TREE

LOWER LAWN

LOW SHRUBS

FRAME

SEED BED

FENCE

GRASS BANK

DOWN

PATH

BOWLS

FLOWERS

EXTRA PAVING

EXISTING PAVING

SEAT

FLAGSTONES

CORDON FRUIT

LAWN

SHRUBS

EXISTING WORKSHOP

FLOWERS

CLIMBERS

GARAGE

HOUSE

54'

30

5

Existing paths
BOREHAM, ESSEX

Many small gardens consist of a lawn, with a central path and narrow flower borders round the boundaries. They may be very colourful and in perfect condition, but they are not very exciting. If it is not desirable or possible to remove the path it can be made less obvious by incorporating it in a larger area of paving.

This garden gets plenty of morning sunshine on the east-facing concrete, but by the time that the commuter husband arrives home, most of the garden is in deep shade.

A circle of paving in the north-east corner breaks the straight line of the existing path and forms a sunny sitting out place, backed by shrubs. An informal pool adds considerable interest, while a border for roses outlining the paving gives a sense of seclusion.

Shrubs give added privacy right along the east and south boundaries. A bold planting of flowers brightens the front of the south boundary shrub border. Flowers also flank the west side of the paved circle.

A small flowering tree, set on paving, in the south-east corner is balanced by a similar tree, or a small conifer which screens out the back of the garage, as seen from the seat.

Low-growing heaths soften the angle of the existing path, and the whole arrangement gives a very pleasant lawn shape, disguising the square outlines of the plot.

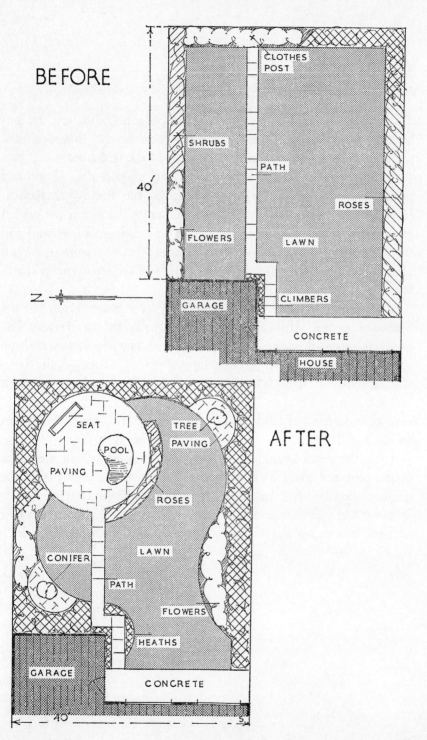

BEFORE

CLOTHES POST

SHRUBS

PATH

40'

ROSES

FLOWERS

LAWN

N

GARAGE

CLIMBERS

CONCRETE

HOUSE

SEAT

TREE
PAVING

AFTER

POOL

PAVING

ROSES

CONIFER

LAWN

PATH

FLOWERS

HEATHS

GARAGE

CONCRETE

40

5

93

Screening from neighbours
CLEVEDON, SOMERSET

This garden is on a corner site and has two neighbouring gardens backing on to its south side. There is also another house on the north side, so the whole garden is in view, back and front.

A continuous high fence would cut out a good deal of air and sunshine and give an enclosed feeling to the narrowing garden. However, an ample terrace with a step down to the rest of the garden gives slight seclusion to the lawn, while an existing six-foot wall and shrub planting on the east side give some privacy from the open planning of the front gardens, and make a sheltered corner for a few salads, near the house.

A hedge to the south side, with a row of summer beans for the first year or so, will give privacy eventually to the terrace. The hedge is repeated at the far end of the garden, but a curved shrub border in between gives greater interest to the shape of the lawn and screens out the ends of the neighbouring gardens and their probable compost heaps.

A neat corner is found for the children with a wendy house, set on paving and given its own private entrance between shrub plantings.

Along the north boundary, cordon fruit takes up little of the width of the plot and gives immediate and permanent screening from the neighbouring house and garden. With small bulbs in a narrow border at their feet, cordons make a charming spring picture; their ease of maintenance makes them an ideal way of growing fruit in a small garden.

SCREENING FROM NEIGHBOURS

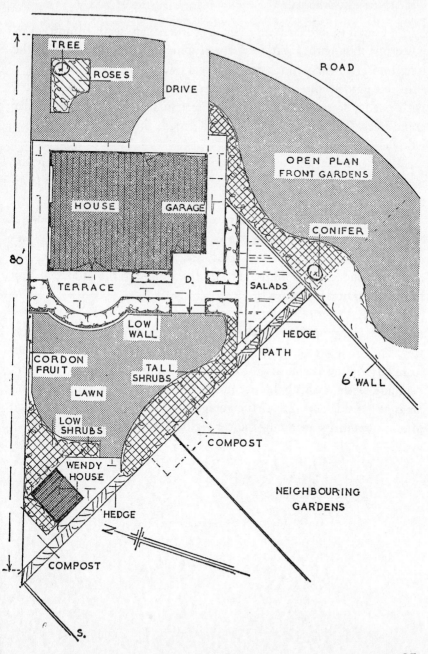

TREE

ROSES

DRIVE

ROAD

OPEN PLAN
FRONT GARDENS

HOUSE

GARAGE

CONIFER

80'

TERRACE

D.

SALADS

LOW
WALL

HEDGE

PATH

CORDON
FRUIT

TALL
SHRUBS

6' WALL

LAWN

LOW
SHRUBS

COMPOST

WENDY
HOUSE

NEIGHBOURING
GARDENS

HEDGE

N

COMPOST

S.

An existing orchard
UPMINSTER, ESSEX

Part of an old orchard in a small garden can seem almost over-powering, but with a little expert pruning to bring the best of the trees into good shape, they can be a real asset to the garden layout.

In this garden, the ragged grass bank is straightened up and flanked with paving to make a setting for a seat in the shade of the smaller apple trees. The existing shed is linked with the new paving to give a tidy effect.

Shrubs give shelter to the seat on the north side, replacing the narrow perennial border. Flowers are now planted farther away from the shade of the orchard and more on view from the house.

A shrub border, replacing the compost heap, gives privacy down the south boundary as far as the existing evergreen hedge, (*Chamaecyparis lawsoniana*), and a fine central pear tree is used as a focal point and surrounded by a raised flower bed, linking the informal and formal parts of the garden.

The small area of paving near the living-room doors is increased to give a large patio, incorporating the existing flowering cherry tree, and giving dignity to this part of the garden to offset the informality of the orchard. Flower borders outline the new patio and combine with a shrub border to screen out the rearranged utility areas at the side and rear of the garage. The front garden is simplified to allow room for bringing the car right up to the front door.

BEFORE

AND

AFTER →

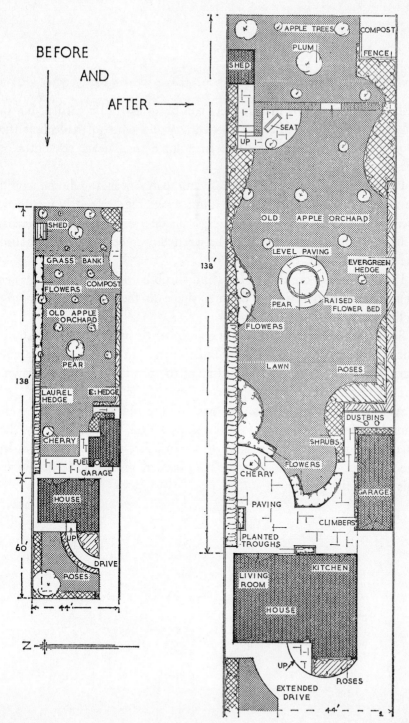

Z

Two trees
INGRAVE, ESSEX

A fine background of mature trees can be an asset to a garden, but in this case they are in the south boundary and tend to shade half the plot. In addition, there are two fine apple trees near the centre of the site.

However, as the large, south-facing patio near the house could be almost overpowering in real summer weather, a seat is included, facing west. Set in a recess amongst shade-loving flowering shrubs, it has a view across the garden between flower beds grouped behind the two apple trees.

Paving outlines the flower beds and shrub border, making for easier management and giving a definite shape to the grass walk leading to the seat.

Seen from the patio, the bright colours of the flowers and the sharp lines of the paving show up behind the straight trunks of the apple trees. Rose borders soften the outline of the patio as it meets the lawn, and two flower beds break up the expanse of the paving squares.

A line of paving neatens the base of the old hedge on the west boundary and gives access to the compost area, screened out by the shade-loving shrubs, and a small flowering shrub, set on the lawn in the curve of the east boundary shrub border, gives a little height to this part of the garden.

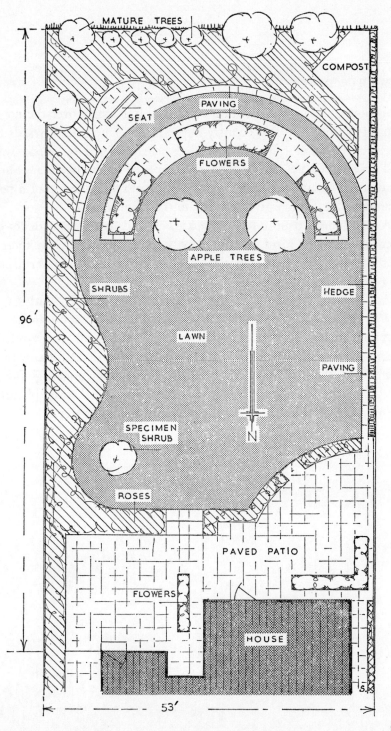

MATURE TREES

COMPOST

PAVING

SEAT

FLOWERS

APPLE TREES

SHRUBS

HEDGE

LAWN

PAVING

N

SPECIMEN SHRUB

ROSES

PAVED PATIO

FLOWERS

HOUSE

96'

53'

View across the garden
LOUGHTON, ESSEX

This house, the next to last in a cul-de-sac, has a view over the neighbouring garden to open country beyond. The land rises towards the north, so a circular lawn is planned here, retained by coped walls and surrounded by rose beds. A seat, recessed in the boundary shrub border, has an uninterrupted view to the south over the top of a new, prunus hedge, which gives privacy to the neighbours.

A wide-paved patio outside the kitchen and living-room doors has been extended to form a dining out section, pleasant when there is evening sunlight. This is flanked by screen walling and shrub and flower planting.

An existing ornament in the west corner is retained and set on paving, backed by the formal hedge screening the compost area.

A perennial border gives colour to the forefront of the view from the seat. The path which leads to the compost, also make for easy management of the back of the flower border. Stepping stones, giving an outline to the lawn, together with some low ground-cover planting, help to tidy up the area under the large existing apple tree.

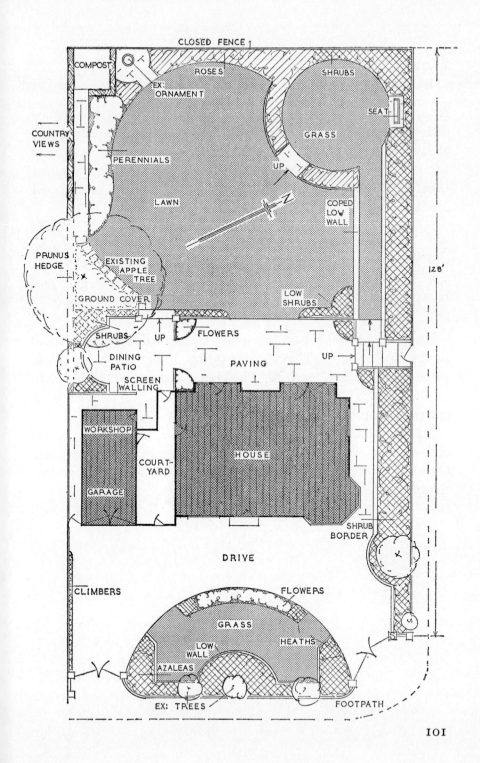

CLOSED FENCE

COMPOST

EX: ORNAMENT

ROSES

SHRUBS

SEAT

COUNTRY VIEWS

PERENNIALS

GRASS

LAWN

UP

COPED LOW WALL

PRUNUS HEDGE

EXISTING APPLE TREE

GROUND COVER

LOW SHRUBS

SHRUBS

UP

FLOWERS

DINING PATIO

UP

PAVING

SCREEN WALLING

WORKSHOP

COURT-YARD

HOUSE

GARAGE

SHRUB BORDER

DRIVE

CLIMBERS

FLOWERS

GRASS

LOW WALL

HEATHS

AZALEAS

EX: TREES

FOOTPATH

128'

101

Distant views
CHIGWELL, ESSEX

A lovely view of a golf course is the main attraction of this garden site. An ample paved patio is placed centrally, facing the open expanse of lawn leading up to the end of the garden, where the two-strand wire fence is the only boundary indication. A revolving summer house in the far corner commands a view of both garden and golf course.

To create more interest near the house a paved walk leads up from the patio, through flower or low shrub borders, to a circular pool with a central fountain jet. This is backed by a border for floribunda and climbing roses, curved back to give ample room for formal beds for H. T. roses, without detracting from the open view up the lawn.

Large neighbouring trees and old established flowering trees and shrubs on the west side are brightened by making room for flower planting in a curve, extending the border beyond the shade of the existing trees. This would be cheerful as seen from the summer house and from the patio.

An island bed for low shrubs screens out the old compost area and adds a touch of colour to break the prevailing green effect, without obstructing the view. Room is found for a sandpit, set in paving, near the house window.

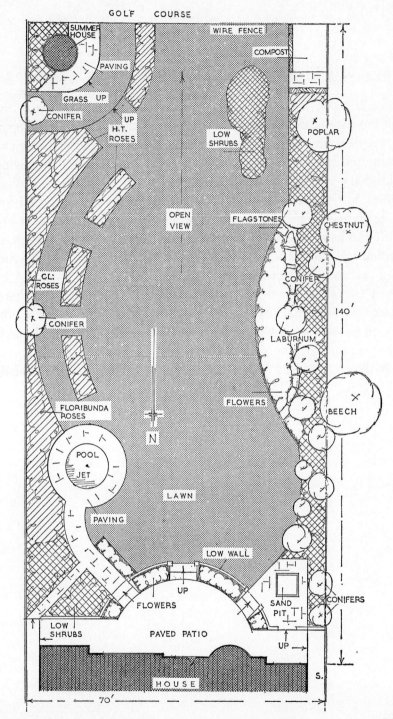

GOLF COURSE

SUMMER HOUSE

PAVING

GRASS UP

CONIFER

UP H.T. ROSES

WIRE FENCE

COMPOST

LOW SHRUBS

POPLAR

OPEN VIEW

FLAGSTONES

CHESTNUT

CONIFER

CL: ROSES

140'

CONIFER

LABURNUM

FLORIBUNDA ROSES

FLOWERS

BEECH

N

POOL & JET

PAVING

LAWN

LOW WALL

UP

FLOWERS

SAND PIT

CONIFERS

LOW SHRUBS

PAVED PATIO

UP

S.

HOUSE

70'

103

Overlooking a brook
HENFIELD, SUSSEX

A small brook at the end of this garden and existing hedgerow trees call for an informal design. A curved paved area, reached by stepping stones through a grass walk, overlooks the brook and distant views. Rockwork is built up against a retaining wall, outlining the paving. This makes a setting for an informal pool.

Nearer the house it was felt that some privacy was needed and more formality. Formal rose beds grouped around an ornament link with the house door and windows, and are softened by the curved outline of a shrub border, which also forms a setting for the informal pool as seen from the paving.

An area to the south side of the house is developed as a sheltered flower garden, catching all the morning sunshine. A seat in this section has a view, across the lawn, to flowers backed by the shrubs of the south boundary border.

A flowering cherry on the lawn helps to balance the height of the tall existing trees on the far boundary.

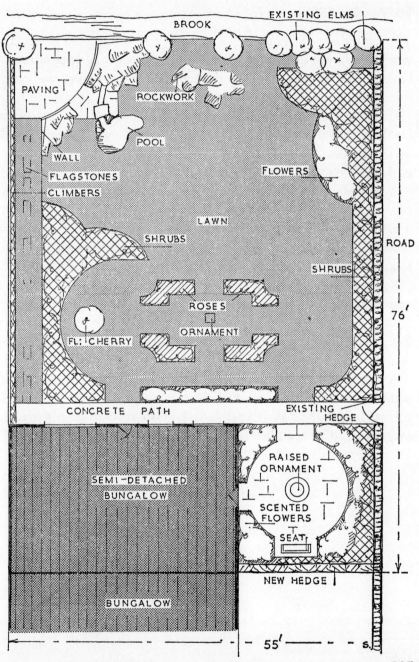

N

BROOK

EXISTING ELMS

PAVING

ROCKWORK

POOL

WALL

FLAGSTONES

CLIMBERS

FLOWERS

LAWN

SHRUBS

SHRUBS

ROSES

ORNAMENT

FL: CHERRY

CONCRETE PATH

EXISTING
HEDGE

ROAD

76'

SEMI-DETACHED
BUNGALOW

RAISED
ORNAMENT

SCENTED
FLOWERS

SEAT

BUNGALOW

NEW HEDGE

55'   s.

105

Part of an old garden
HUTTON, ESSEX

This bungalow was built to the south side of a large old house. The new boundary is defined by a spindly privet hedge. A series of linked, broken concrete pools took up the centre of the new plot, and ended in a concrete-walled compost area.

Concrete near the bungalow is curved to follow the lines of the building, and softened by being outlined with flower borders. Breaks in the borders give access to the lawn, and one allows room for a bird table—on view from the kitchen window.

A curved path runs between flower borders, disguising the line of the privet hedge. This leads to a seat, set in a walled recess and with a view across the rock garden which has been formed on the site of the old pools. Steps lead down into the rock garden and up again to a path, past the compost area, to a small area for salads and fruit.

Beyond the seat, curved shrub borders break the line of the privet and combine with an island bed and a specimen tree to make a setting for daffodils, naturalised in the grass, where their fading foliage will not be an eyesore from the bungalow windows. The trees established in the garden of the large house make a fine background.

A large overhanging oak tree near the house makes boundary shrub planting unsatisfactory, so small bulbs are naturalised to give early colour, before the oak is in full leaf. Two small specimen trees, a magnolia and an acer, break the expanse of the main lawn.

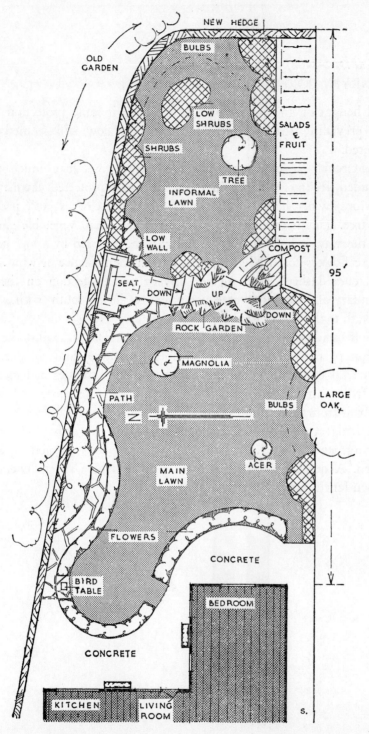

NEW HEDGE

OLD GARDEN

BULBS

LOW SHRUBS

SHRUBS

TREE

INFORMAL LAWN

SALADS & FRUIT

LOW WALL

COMPOST

SEAT

DOWN

UP

DOWN

ROCK GARDEN

95'

MAGNOLIA

PATH

BULBS

LARGE OAK

N

MAIN LAWN

ACER

FLOWERS

CONCRETE

BIRD TABLE

CONCRETE

BEDROOM

KITCHEN

LIVING ROOM

S.

107

A wind-swept garden
PENRYN, CORNWALL

Old hedges on three sides of this site gave it some protection from the prevailing strong winds, but the bungalow still seemed very exposed.

A circular arrangement of rose borders gives it a much more secluded feeling and provides several small protected lawns. The previous owner had laid a path as far as the clothes post, past the old tree. This is extended to give access to a small vegetable garden. On the way, it links with a formal garden, enclosed by a low hedge, where flowers could be grown away from the nuisance of wind.

A curved shrub border gives privacy and protection on the east boundary and shields a recess for a seat set facing south, with a view through to the flower garden.

Half-standard and pyramid fruit trees are planted against the protection of the old hedge on the north boundary and smaller, soft bush fruit in the sheltered north-west corner. Lavender hedges flank the front entrance path and combine with the rose borders to screen the fruit from the windows of the bungalow.

If hedges are required and do not exist it is worth erecting low fencing, such as wattle, while young hedge plants are getting established. A quicker alternative to hedging is double ranch fencing or woven fencing covered with climbers.

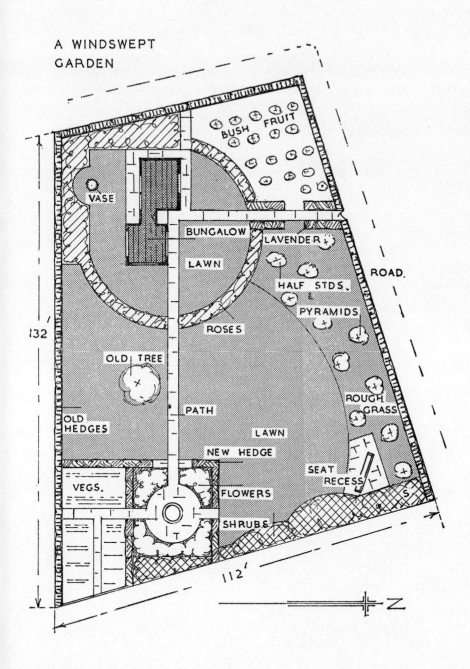

A WINDSWEPT
GARDEN

BUSH FRUIT

VASE

BUNGALOW

LAVENDER

LAWN

HALF STDS.

PYRAMIDS

ROSES

ROAD.

132

OLD TREE

ROUGH
GRASS

PATH

OLD
HEDGES

LAWN

NEW HEDGE

VEGS.

SEAT
RECESS

FLOWERS

S

SHRUBS

112'

N

6 Dealing with levels

Nothing creates so much interest in a garden as a variation in levels, however slight. People with flat sites long to raise or sink some part. Those with sloping sites are often very worried about how to set about planning their uneven garden.

A steep slope up from the back of the house can be very frustrating, especially if it means that the windows of the house have no clear view of the garden.

It is wise to keep the necessary bank or wall as many feet away from the house as possible, especially opposite a door or window. Wide, ample steps in the wall will help to open up the view of the garden. Alpine planting in the face of the wall, rather than on the top, and a border for vivid seasonal planting at the base of the wall will help to counteract the overpowering enclosing effect of the rising garden beyond.

Where the main fall is across the garden it is interesting to be able to form a terrace effect to one side. One of the problems will be privacy, but this can be overcome by wise planting.

Planting has a lot to do with the success of a well planned garden on varying levels. Shrubs are needed for a permanent effect to soften any harshness of the necessary retaining walls. Trees are useful for giving focal points linking the various parts of the garden, and also for height to balance the varying proportions. It is very important to check on the ultimate height and spread of such permanent material. It becomes as much part of the garden design as the structural materials used and will help to form the final outline of the garden picture.

This becomes apparent with land falling away from the back of the house. It gives scope for a very pleasant garden, arranged in sections, with varying interests from one level to the other but without careful planting there is little to see from the house windows.

On a flat site a lot can be done to create a three-dimensional effect by the use of island beds of shrubs or perennials. If rockwork is needed it is worth building up a rough wall to form a definite rock bank, rather than having an unsatisfactory mound. With a new site it may be possible to have a slightly sunken lawn and then use the excavated soil to give a raised terrace.

By thinking about the plan early enough it may be possible to have the builder's debris and sub-soil put just where it can be used to make the garden shape more interesting. A pond or a swimming pool can give plenty of excavated soil to form grass- or shrub-planted banks, to provide a good deal of unexpected privacy to a flat site.

Sloping down to the house
VERYAN, CORNWALL

The large kitchen window of this old house faces north and looks onto a four-foot high grey stone wall nine feet away, with rising lawn beyond it and tall trees on the skyline. A border for low, vivid flowers and a few dwarf conifers for winter contrast is planted at the base of the wall. This gives interest without making the kitchen feel even more enclosed.

At the top of the steps, paths link the various outbuildings, and a paved extension to these gives a sitting area which catches the morning sun. A few flowers here and a small island bed for low-growing heaths gives extra brightness to the kitchen view without blocking the open expanse of lawn.

As new bungalows have been built beyond the west boundary, the garden has been adapted to give the necessary privacy and make an interesting shape to the lawn. Curved shrub borders are brought well out from the north-west boundary line of the Cornish hedge to make for easier maintenance. Tough, wind-resistant shrubs at the back of these borders allow for a little flower planting to the east sides, giving colour across the lawn as seen from the kitchen.

Existing fruit trees have been maintained to help shield the upper, exposed part of the garden from the wind. A raised seat is included in the north-east corner, where it gets plenty of sunshine and a view of the sea.

Naturalised bulbs in the shrub borders and around the two old trees on the lawn make this garden a delight during the early days of spring.

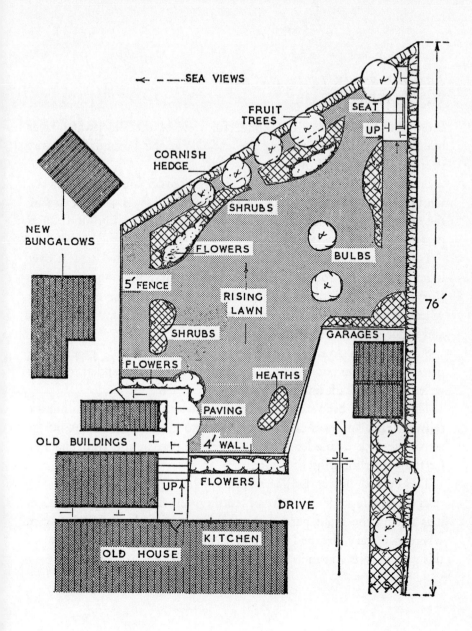

SEA VIEWS

FRUIT TREES

SEAT

UP

CORNISH HEDGE

SHRUBS

FLOWERS

BULBS

NEW BUNGALOWS

5' FENCE

RISING LAWN

SHRUBS

GARAGES

FLOWERS

HEATHS

PAVING

N

OLD BUILDINGS

4' WALL

UP

FLOWERS

DRIVE

KITCHEN

OLD HOUSE

76'

Falling away from the house
WEST MERSEA, ESSEX

From this house there is a wonderful view of the Blackwater river but very little can be seen of the garden, as the ground falls away steeply, down to the beach.

Below the terrace by the house, there is a border for scented flowers, flanking a level lawn, which is taken out as far as possible before the necessary retaining wall. The wall forms a background for a paved rose terrace, with a recess for a seat overlooking the water.

The second retaining wall has climbing roses planted to fall over it and clothe the south face of the wall as it flanks another lawn. Curved steps lead down to this section, with a summer house set where it has a view of the distant water, and also a view of the rock and water garden at its feet.

Straight steps from the rose terrace give access to a greenhouse, placed so that the power cable for heating it can be extended to pump water for the cascade and pools of the rock garden.

This area had been excavated by the previous owner for a miniature railway track and was easily converted into a water garden. A bridge across the rock ravine leads to the vegetable garden and an open space for the winter mooring of a boat.

The curved flower border screening the vegetable garden path is reserved mainly for flowers for cutting for floral arrangements, as it is not on the main garden view. Privacy from the public is given, where necessary, by hedging and trees, but one of the delights of this garden is its charm as seen from the beach.

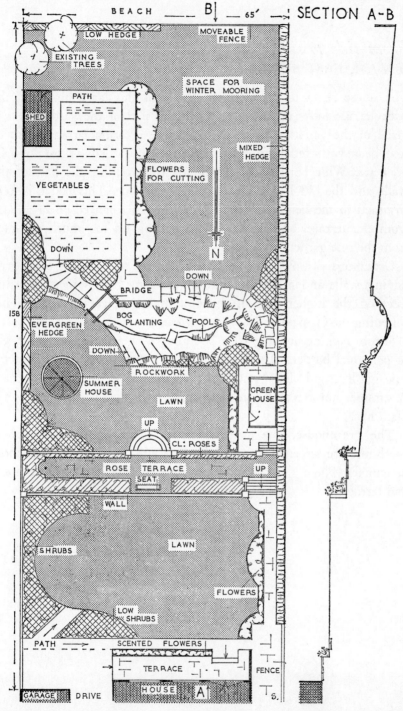

BEACH   B↓ — 65′ —↓   SECTION A-B

LOW HEDGE   MOVEABLE FENCE

EXISTING TREES

SPACE FOR WINTER MOORING

PATH

SHED

MIXED HEDGE

FLOWERS FOR CUTTING

VEGETABLES

N

DOWN

158

DOWN

BRIDGE

BOG PLANTING   POOLS

EVERGREEN HEDGE

DOWN

ROCKWORK

SUMMER HOUSE

LAWN

GREEN HOUSE

UP

CL: ROSES

ROSE TERRACE

SEAT

UP

WALL

LAWN

SHRUBS

FLOWERS

LOW SHRUBS

PATH →   SCENTED FLOWERS

TERRACE

FENCE

GARAGE   DRIVE   HOUSE   A   S.

From side to side
HORAM, EAST SUSSEX

The house is set to the south-west side of this large plot, and the wide terrace looks down on to the lower part of the garden. Use is made of the variation in levels to enclose a formal arrangement of rose beds with retaining walls, cutting the garden almost in half, sideways. Wide borders for floribunda roses outline the base of the walls and the old hedge on the south-west side. This hedge is kept trimmed to the height of the walls to give a balanced effect as seen from the terrace, and also to avoid cutting off too much sunshine from the rose garden.

Groupings of low-growing shrubs soften the corners of the retaining walls and make a frame for the long rose borders. Existing trees on the higher part of the plot make a pleasant background, softening the formality of the rose garden.

Shrub planting at the garden boundary corners is linked by lengths of perennial borders. These give colour as seen from the steps of the rose garden, and also as seen on the far boundary from the terrace. A summer house recessed in the east corner is flanked by these flower plantings.

The greenhouse, shed, vegetables and general utility areas near the house are screened by shrub borders and an island bed for more perennials. These give added colour as seen from the summer house and terrace.

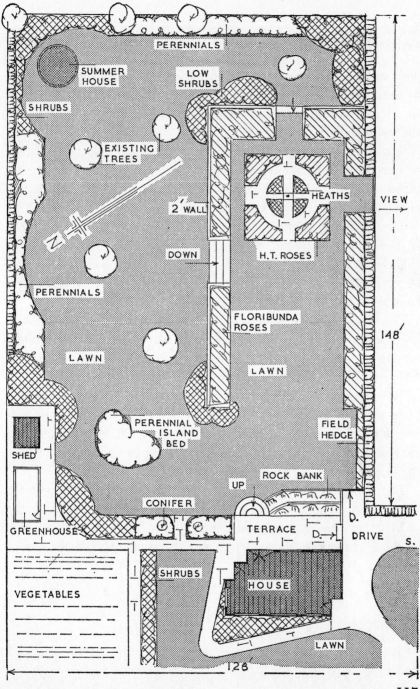

PERENNIALS

SUMMER HOUSE

LOW SHRUBS

SHRUBS

EXISTING TREES

HEATHS

VIEW

2' WALL

DOWN

H.T. ROSES

PERENNIALS

FLORIBUNDA ROSES

148'

LAWN

LAWN

PERENNIAL ISLAND BED

FIELD HEDGE

SHED

ROCK BANK

UP

GREENHOUSE

CONIFER

TERRACE

D.

DRIVE

S.

SHRUBS

VEGETABLES

HOUSE

LAWN

128'

Cross Falls
LOUGHTON ESSEX

This small garden has the disadvantage of a ten-foot drop from north to south and a slight fall from west to east. The bonus is that from the shaped terrace there is a magnificent view right over the top of the east boundary fence.

Steps from the terrace are kept well to the sides rather than central, to save cutting into the narrowness of the lawn. For the same reason, planting on the east boundary is kept just to climbers, sufficient to clothe the woven fencing, without obstructing the view.

The steep rise to the north under the existing beech and birch is reserved for the children's play area. Grass sown, and still sloping slightly, it is arranged in two levels with a grass bank and simple steps. Planting on the north and east boundaries of the children's lawn gives colour as seen from the house.

There are curved steps down from the children's area to the lower lawn and also formal steps, connecting with the terrace. The simple, curved retaining wall has matt alpine planting at the top, allowed to fall over and soften the south face of the wall.

The depression in the south-east corner of the garden is the only place to catch the evening sunshine, so a level paving, or grass area here for sitting out is surrounded by trough retaining walls allowing for rose planting. A small flowering tree in the corner helps to balance the height of the two existing trees and screens nearby houses.

The path from the sitting out area rises gently up towards the terrace and ends in formal steps. Two small conifers flanking the steps set off the terrace against the dignity of the Georgian house in the background. Shrubs screen out the rising base of the terrace wall on the east side.

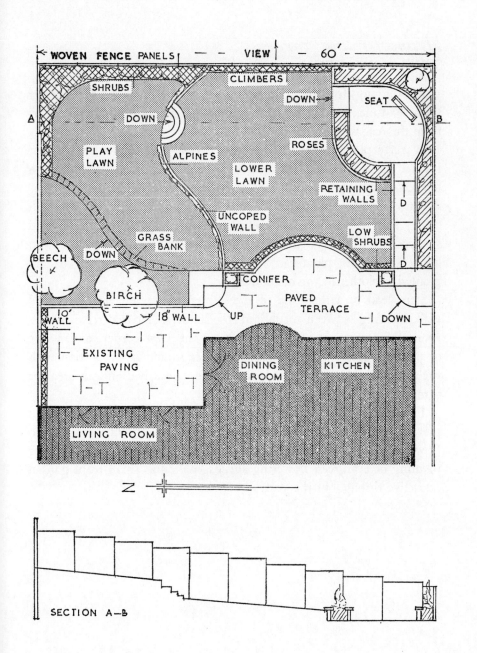

WOVEN FENCE PANELS — — VIEW — 60'
SHRUBS
CLIMBERS
DOWN
SEAT
A
DOWN
B
PLAY
LAWN
ALPINES
LOWER
LAWN
ROSES
RETAINING
WALLS
D
UNCOPED
WALL
GRASS
BANK
DOWN
LOW
SHRUBS
D
BEECH
CONIFER
BIRCH
PAVED
TERRACE
10'
WALL
18" WALL
UP
DOWN
EXISTING
PAVING
DINING
ROOM
KITCHEN
LIVING ROOM

N

SECTION A—B

119

A small rising garden
SEVENOAKS, KENT

After digging for the foundations of this bungalow, the builder proposed to leave a soil bank, two-and-a-half-feet high, three feet away from the rear windows of the building,

By early planning, the owner was able to arrange for him to cut further back into the land and so give a level lawn, extending to ten feet away from his proposed three-feet-wide concrete path.

It was then possible to have a curved retaining wall, which although nearly four feet high, is well away from the bungalow windows and shelters a secluded lawn. Crevices left in the east face of the wall allow for alpine planting. Prostrate and low growing shrubs are planted to clothe the top of the wall.

Steps lead up either side of the garden to a wide grass or paved walk, curving between shrub and rose borders. A paved recess allows room for a seat, set high up in the sunny west corner, and a line of pyramid-grown fruit trees gives a background in proportion with the levels of the site, and helps to screen a seed bed and an area for compost.

The sunny front of this bungalow has a loggia which is given privacy from the road by a bold planting of floribunda roses. Two flowering trees, chosen for spring and autumn effect, and a corner planting of evergreen flowering shrubs, make this small front garden attractive throughout the year.

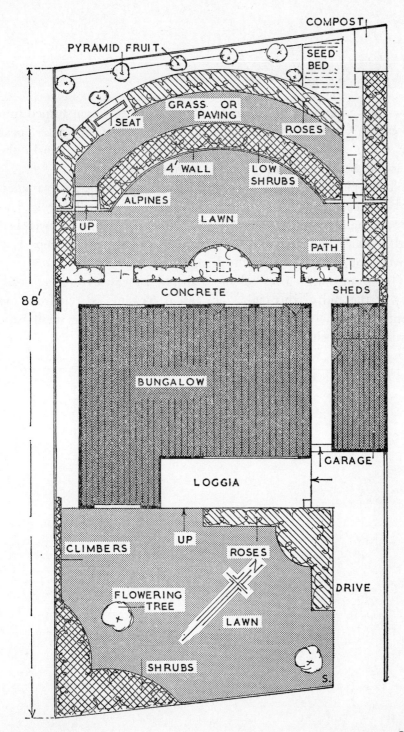

COMPOST

PYRAMID FRUIT

SEED BED

GRASS OR PAVING

SEAT

ROSES

4' WALL

LOW SHRUBS

ALPINES

LAWN

UP

PATH

CONCRETE

SHEDS

BUNGALOW

GARAGE

LOGGIA

UP

CLIMBERS

ROSES

FLOWERING TREE

DRIVE

LAWN

SHRUBS

S.

88'

A sloping front garden
LOUGHTON, ESSEX

The dull grass bank at the front of this house has been turned into an exciting rock garden. A stepped wall, starting at three feet near the house and dropping to nothing at the road edge, marks the boundary between the neighbouring front garden.

Shrub planting, including some flowering evergreen varieties, makes a background for curved, rising paved walks. These lead to a level, half-moon paved area, where there is a raised flower bed and a small flowering tree or ornament. Wide central steps lead down through rock banks to the drive level.

The arrangement gives colour to the rather vast expanse of roadway at the end of this cul-de-sac, and is pleasing as seen from the front door and main living-room window. It leaves the small back garden free for children's games.

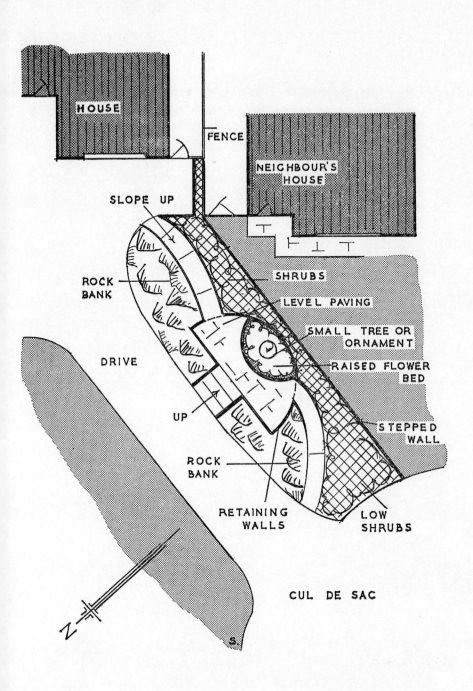

HOUSE

FENCE

NEIGHBOUR'S
HOUSE

SLOPE UP

ROCK
BANK

SHRUBS

LEVEL PAVING

SMALL TREE OR
ORNAMENT

RAISED FLOWER
BED

DRIVE

UP

STEPPED
WALL

ROCK
BANK

RETAINING
WALLS

LOW
SHRUBS

CUL DE SAC

N S

123

7 Individual needs

Different households make different demands on their garden space, and these personal preferences and requirements help to suggest its design.

Some want a garden which is always neat and tidy. Others prefer one which grows and seeds at will. Some have to cater for the needs of children or pets, while others look to the garden to give them a constant supply of fruit and vegetables, or flowers for floral decoration. A good many people like to include water in some way, either formal or informal.

Place has to be found for favourite plants such as dahlias, chrysanthemums, irises, roses and flowering trees and shrubs.

For the dedicated gardener, finding space for children's activities is a real problem. For a few years it is best to compromise. Allocate a definite section, if possible, for ball games, and screen it with a line of tough shrubs or even blackcurrant bushes. Later on this area might be adapted as a place for a barbecue, and later still as a secluded sitting out place.

Try to arrange the main flower display where it will take least damage from balls and trampling feet. A flat stone on a border making one way—and one way only—across will save erratic damage. Concentrate on compact plants and avoid, for the time being, plants such as gladioli and tall dahlias which can be ruined for the season in a split second.

To be a worth-while extension to the home, a garden should have at least one sheltered place where immediate advantage can be taken of the odd spells of sunshine that our climate produces. Ideally this should be near the house doors, but if this is an area which doesn't get sunshine at the time of day you are usually free to enjoy it, try to arrange a sitting out place in some other part of the garden. Make sure that it is easily accessible by a firm path and if it is too far to carry out temporary garden furniture, have a permanent seat there.

There are makes which can be shut down when not in use to keep them dry, or it can become second nature to keep a plastic cushion handy by the door, and take it with you.

Dry access is also necessary if you plan to grow vegetables, but this need not be a firm path. A line of flagstones is often sufficient to make work and picking possible immediately after a heavy shower. Service paths should be wide enough to take your wheelbarrow comfortably. Screen the vegetables from the main garden if possible, even if it is only by a line of roses, or cordon fruit, runner beans, sweet peas or raspberries.

Those who prefer a wild, woodland garden often find difficulty in keeping it reasonably tidy all through the year, once the spring glory has passed. However, large flat flagstones forming curved walks through it, or even wide grass walks cut occasionally with the mower, will suggest shape to the layout and give the area some look of purpose. Ground-cover planting outlining the path can give colour and leaf shape at the side of the walks and obscure the unavoidable disorder under the trees.

If you keep a picture in your mind's eye of what you are aiming at, you will be able to ensure that your garden suits the needs of your household, over the passing years.

Room for hobbies
WARRINGTON, LANCASHIRE

This design allows room for many varied hobbies, and while being decorative, is also highly practical. All the planting, for example, can be maintained easily from flagstone paths, flowing unobtrusively in front or behind borders. The odd shape of the plot aids this layout, and it is certainly the sort of site which is best worked out on paper, before starting constructional work.

Narrow concrete paths gave little room round the kitchen door, so these have been widened into a semi-circle, which now links three paths and is screened from the main lawn by a rose border.

The new path to the north gives direct access to the owner's aviary, fitted in behind the garage. It continues behind a seat set in the recess of a shrub border, to lead to the compost, vegetable and soft fruit

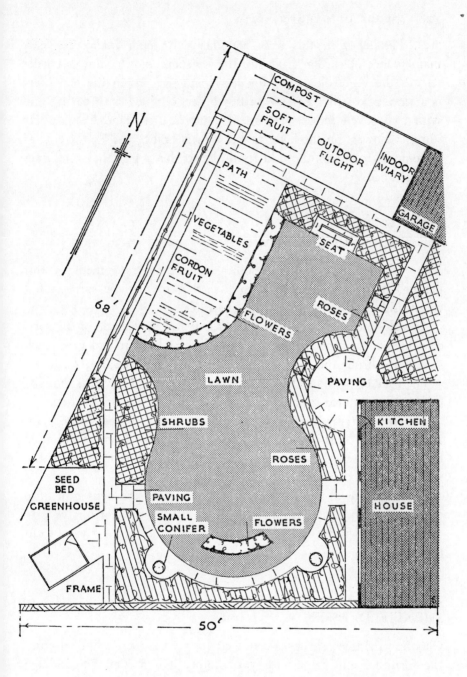

N

COMPOST

SOFT FRUIT

OUTDOOR FLIGHT

INDOOR AVIARY

GARAGE

PATH

VEGETABLES

CORDON FRUIT

SEAT

FLOWERS

ROSES

68'

LAWN

PAVING

SHRUBS

ROSES

SEED BED

GREENHOUSE

PAVING

SMALL CONIFER

FLOWERS

KITCHEN

HOUSE

FRAME

50'

area. Parallel with the west boundary, the path makes for easy maintenance of cordon fruit and the vegetable plot. A flower border screens the vegetables from the lawn and seat. From the seat there is a view across the lawn to a rose border, outlined with paving and with two paved recesses for small conifers. An island bed for gay summer flowers on the lawn makes a focal point.

Room is found in the odd south corner for a greenhouse, frames and seed bed.

Overlooking a riding school
WEST HANNINGFIELD, ESSEX

The activities of a riding school govern the arrangement of this garden. It is planned to be decorative, but part of the surrounding countryside, and as labour-saving as possible.

A wide entrance and drive give room for movement of all sorts of vehicles. The appearance is softened by areas of mown grass each side, with shrubs and trees set in rough grass for necessary screening.

The back of the house faces north but gets enough sunshine to make this a safe play area for small children, in view from the kitchen.

The main living-room doors face east, and a paved patio is introduced here. This is given a sense of seclusion by being surrounded by a low retaining wall, coped and with piers, linking it with the architecture of the house.

Beyond the wall, a grass walk and circular rose beds fade into the open fields of the riding school. Shrubs to the north give protection from winds, and roses to the south side give privacy from the drive.

A plantsman's garden
SHENFIELD, ESSEX

Choosing the trees, shrubs and flowers for your garden is like selecting the furniture and carpets for your home. It is a chance to indulge your own tastes. Experts may suggest and advise, but it is worth acquiring as much knowledge as you can for yourself. *You* have to live with the final results.

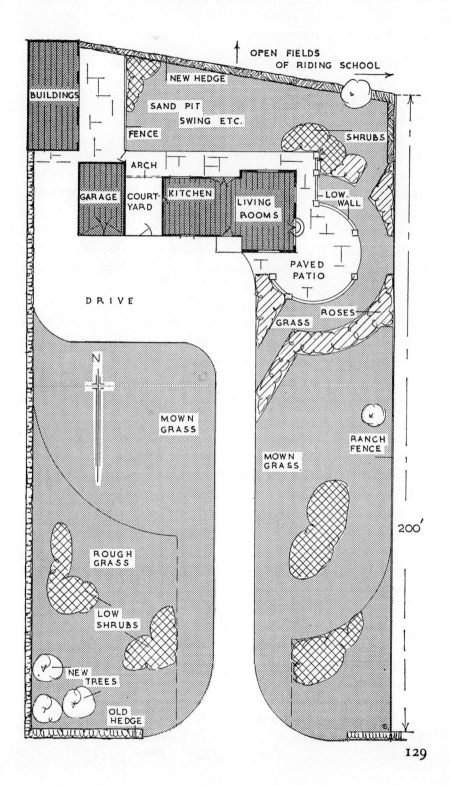

OPEN FIELDS
OF RIDING SCHOOL

BUILDINGS

NEW HEDGE

SAND PIT
SWING ETC.

FENCE

SHRUBS

ARCH

GARAGE

COURT-YARD

KITCHEN

LIVING ROOMS

LOW WALL

PAVED PATIO

DRIVE

N

MOWN GRASS

GRASS

ROSES

MOWN GRASS

RANCH FENCE

ROUGH GRASS

LOW SHRUBS

NEW TREES

OLD HEDGE

200'

Plants can be studied, and their names become slightly more familiar, by browsing through nurserymen's catalogues and garden centres. You can see the plants growing more naturally in public gardens, or enjoy the perfect specimens at the Royal Horticultural Society flower shows. Here, everything is labelled meticulously, and you can study new introductions.

Be adventurous. Don't be content with the everyday varieties if something sturdier and more free-flowering has been introduced long enough ago to be reasonable in price.

You may suddenly become aware of the glories of one particular group such as lilies, irises, alpines, dahlias, or heaths. Then you find that many plants have flower societies devoted to them, and you enter a new world of exploration.

The amateur owners of this old-fashioned garden realised that, with the shade and leaf fall provided by the mature trees and hedges, their garden was well suited to growing the peat-loving plants such as rhododendrons, camellias, primulas, lilies and bulbs of all kinds.

The design of the garden was opened out a little in several directions to show off new beds and borders across the lawn areas. Several mature shrubs were moved successfully to new positions. This is quite possible with a little extra care and plenty of watering. They then introduced many new shrubs and, over the years, they are developing an oasis of beauty in a built-up commuter area.

Here are the details of their existing planting:

West boundary
1. Silver Birch—60 ft. high
2. *Metasequoia glyptostroboides.* Planted by cutting the old hedge well back. Eventually these trees will replace the birches.

Under pear trees
A. *Ceanothus* 'Gloire de Versailles'
B. *Camellia japonica* 'Nagasaki'
   Underplanting of hostas, ferns and primulas

L-shaped bed

C. *Prunus* 'Shirotae'
D. *Magnolia wilsonii*
E. *Magnolia sargentiana robusta*
F. Holly, variegated
G. *Prunus*, 'Tai Haku'
H. Row of *Paeonia lutea ludlowii*
I. Rose, 'Scented Air'
J. *Cercis siliquastrum*

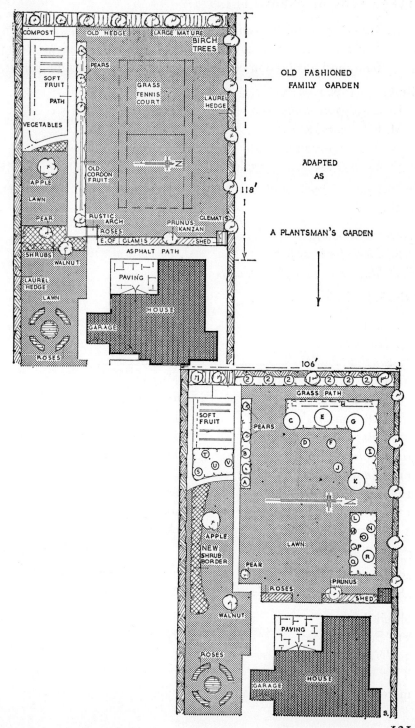

OLD FASHIONED
FAMILY GARDEN

ADAPTED
AS

A PLANTSMAN'S GARDEN

131

K. *Magnolia* × *soulangeana* 'Brozzonii'
Underplanted with cowslips, oxlips, primulas, lilies, spring
bulbs and a collection of Michaelmas daisies for autumn colour.

Rectangular bed

L. *Eucalyptus niphophila*
M. *Viburnum* × *juddii*
N. Rose, 'Queen Elizabeth'
O. *Syringa vulgaris* 'Vestale'

P. *Choisya ternata*
Q. *Hoheria glabrata*
R. *Rhodo. caucasico-pictum*

Underplanted with cistus, heaths, paeonies, lilies and spring
bulbs.

New south boundary shrub border

S. *Pieris formosa forrestii*
T. *Magnolia* × *highdownensis*

U. *Sorbaria aitchisonii*
V. Azaleas

Rhododendrons

3. 'Avalanche'
4. 'Sarita Loder'
5. *vanessa* 'Pastel'
6. *nobleanum* 'Venustum'
7. 'Day Dream'
8. 'C.B. van Nes'
9. 'Polar Bear'
10. *eximium*
11. *quinquefolium*
12. *schlippenbachii*
13. *loderi* 'Pink Diamond'
14. 'Break of Day'

15. *moupinense*
16. 'Seta'
17. 'Praecox'
18. 'May Day'
19. *discolor*
20. 'Red Cap' (Townhill form)
21. *russatum*
22. 'Blue Diamond'
23. *yakushimanum*
24. *wardii*
25. *campylocarpum*
26. 'Albatross'

Camellias

27. 'Leonard Messel'
28. *japonica* 'Nobilissima'

29. *williamsii* 'Donation'
30. 'White Swan'

Shrub Roses

31. 'Frühlingsgold'
32. 'Vanity'

33. 'Nevada'

This part of the border is underplanted with *Cornus canadensis*,
meconopsis, primulas, lilies and spring bulbs.

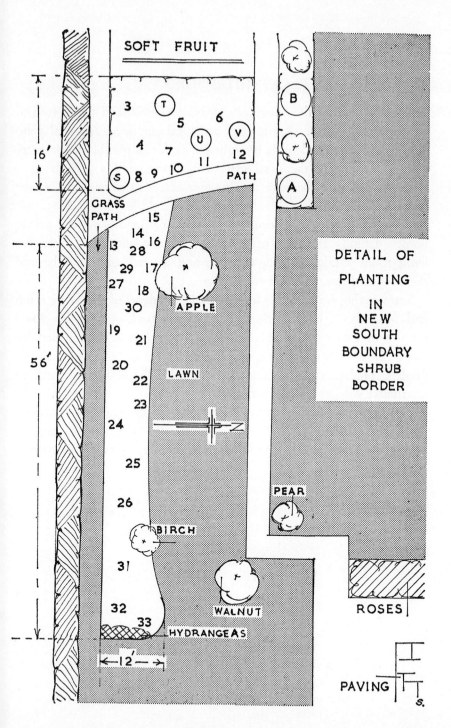

SOFT FRUIT

PATH

GRASS PATH

APPLE

LAWN

N

BIRCH

WALNUT

HYDRANGEAS

←12'→

16'

56'

B

A

PEAR

DETAIL OF
PLANTING
IN
NEW
SOUTH
BOUNDARY
SHRUB
BORDER

ROSES

PAVING

133

A new site
BEACONSFIELD, BUCKINGHAMSHIRE

This new plot had the advantage of existing woodland trees grouped in one corner, where they formed a natural play area. A paved patio outside the kitchen door is brought out as far as possible to be away from the shade of the north-east-facing house, and a path from it curves round past the play area to give access to a gate into a lane beyond the existing laurel hedge.

The path gives a tidy limit to the play area, and a narrow flower border flanking the path helps to obscure any untidyness from the living-room windows. Tough shrubs add a touch of colour beyond the trees, and screen out the compost area.

Extra paving is included outside the sliding doors of the living-room and from this a flower border curves right back against the closed fencing of the north boundary to allow room for an island bed for roses. This helps to give a broader effect to the otherwise square garden. The roses are colourful as seen from the house and form an alternative way around the garden.

The boundary border curves round towards the east and continues as shrub planting to screen out a small salad area, and to make a setting for a seat built around one of the existing trees in this sunnier part of the garden.

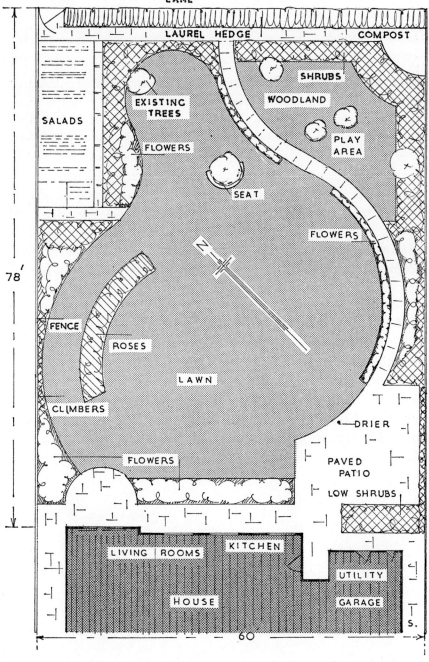

LANE

LAUREL HEDGE   COMPOST

SHRUBS

EXISTING
TREES

WOODLAND

SALADS

FLOWERS

PLAY
AREA

SEAT

FLOWERS

N

FENCE

ROSES

LAWN

CLIMBERS

DRIER

PAVED
PATIO

FLOWERS

LOW SHRUBS

LIVING ROOMS   KITCHEN

HOUSE

UTILITY

GARAGE

S.

78'

60

A country cottage
STOCK, ESSEX

This garden is enclosed by old, well-established boundary hedges, has several old fruit trees and a narrow flower border, with a central arch cutting the garden into two sections. New building beyond the north boundary meant the erection of a high woven fence. A few existing trees help to screen it, but conifers are added to help the winter effect. These then make a setting for a seat, facing south-west and with a view through the arch to the more mature part of the garden.

The dividing flower border is turned, westwards, and developed into a formal arrangement of flower beds grouped around an old weeping ash. This brings the flower display more into view from the large existing terrace and the house windows.

A low prunus hedge backing the flower borders is continued behind the cross borders, and so separates the flower garden from what is now developed as the children's play area. There is plenty of room here for a swing and climbing frame. There is also a small sand pit, set in paving, which continues as a path past the seat and on to give access to the clothes drier and a screened compost area.

The old part of the garden is made more attractive by arranging shrubs round some of the existing big shrubs and planting the area with naturalised bulbs. These are grouped so that their dying foliage is obscured by the spring growth of the more compact, new shrubs.

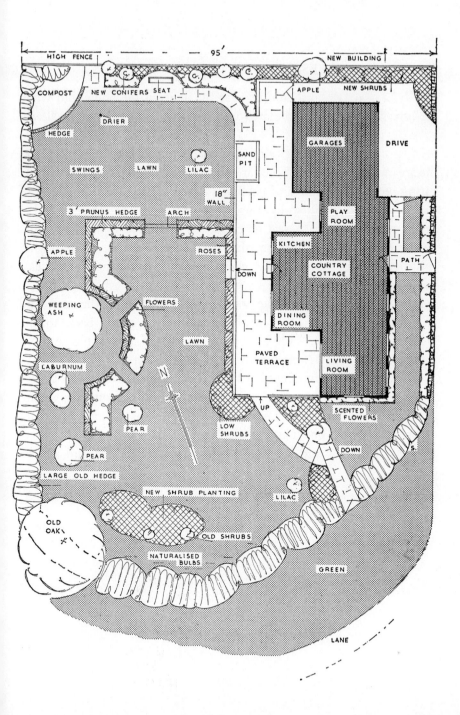

95'

HIGH FENCE · NEW BUILDING

COMPOST · NEW CONIFERS SEAT · APPLE · NEW SHRUBS

HEDGE · DRIER · GARAGES · DRIVE

SWINGS · LAWN · LILAC · SAND PIT

18" WALL · PLAY ROOM

3' PRUNUS HEDGE · ARCH · KITCHEN

ROSES · COUNTRY COTTAGE

APPLE · DOWN · PATH

WEEPING ASH · FLOWERS · DINING ROOM

LABURNUM · LAWN · PAVED TERRACE · LIVING ROOM

N · UP · SCENTED FLOWERS

PEAR · LOW SHRUBS · DOWN · S.

PEAR

LARGE OLD HEDGE · LILAC

NEW SHRUB PLANTING

OLD OAK · OLD SHRUBS

NATURALISED BULBS · GREEN

LANE

137

Sitting out places
HORNCHURCH, ESSEX

Ideally, a paved patio should be near the doors of the house, but when the aspect is due north, the area will get little sunshine and an alternative has to be planned.

In this garden, a large walnut tree tends to add even more shade to the area near the house, so the far end of the site is planned as a definite sitting out place. An area of paving is raised slightly above the level of the lawn, and flanked by raised, square beds for flowers and a small, central conifer. A seat here, backed by climbers and shrubs, has a view across the garden to an island bed for perennials, framed by an existing planting of *cupressocyparis leylandii* on the north and east boundaries.

Low shrub planting to the south gives seclusion to the seat, and an unobtrusive path between the shrubs gives access back to the lawn near the house. This lawn is made as gay as possible by bold rose plantings away from the shade of the walnut.

Use is made of existing paths around the garage to serve a very small vegetable and general utility area, screened from the sitting out area by a curved shrub border, which helps to give a feeling of entrance from one part of the lawn to the other and the effect that the owner wanted—of a quiet retreat at the far end of the garden.

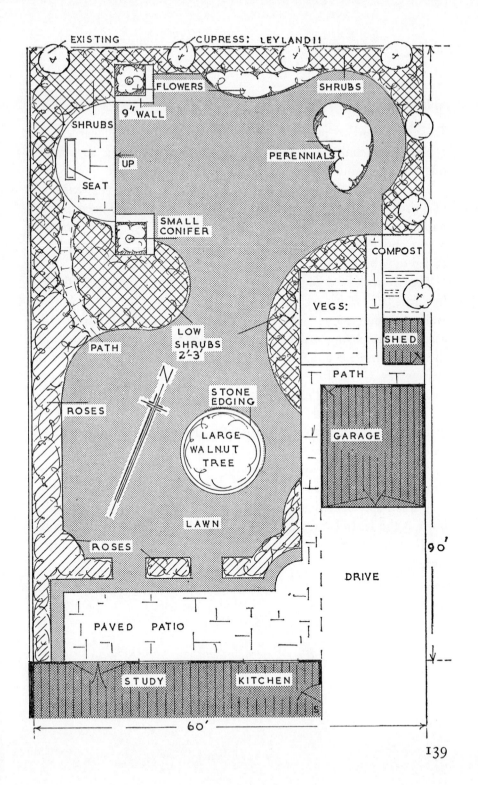

EXISTING   CUPRESS: LEYLAND11

FLOWERS

9" WALL

SHRUBS

UP

SEAT

SMALL
CONIFER

SHRUBS

PERENNIALS

COMPOST

VEGS:

SHED

PATH

LOW
SHRUBS
2'-3'

PATH

ROSES

STONE
EDGING

LARGE
WALNUT
TREE

GARAGE

LAWN

ROSES

90'

DRIVE

PAVED   PATIO

STUDY   KITCHEN

60'

139

A suntrap area
SHENFIELD, ESSEX

Existing boundary planting gave seclusion to this small garden, but robbed it of sunlight, except for the north west corner, so a sitting out place is planned here around an existing walnut tree.

The old laurel hedge on the west boundary has been cut well back. Old shrubs by the conifers on the north boundary have been cleared, and new, colourful flowering shrubs planted, as a background to a seat and to screen out the compost heap. Screen walling could be added as a background to give a more elaborate effect.

The front curved outline of the paved sitting out area is flanked by a rose bed, which continues towards the south to form a double rose walk. Stepping stones lead down the central grass path to give dry access to the paving round the greenhouse and garage and link with the steps outside the door of a sun room extension. The design of the steps gives a graceful treatment to a rather steep drop from house to garden and serves the side entrance as well as the main lawn.

On the east boundary, a tall privet hedge and pollarded limes give privacy to the suntrap area from the neighbouring house, but tend to make the view rather dismal. To offset this, a border is cut in the lawn, well away from the greedy base of the privet, so that gay shrubs and flowers can brighten this part of the garden.

A small specimen shrub, such as an acer, helps to brighten the dull lawn at the foot of the steps, and a semi-circular flower bed screening the base of the greenhouse also adds colour, as seen from the suntrap area.

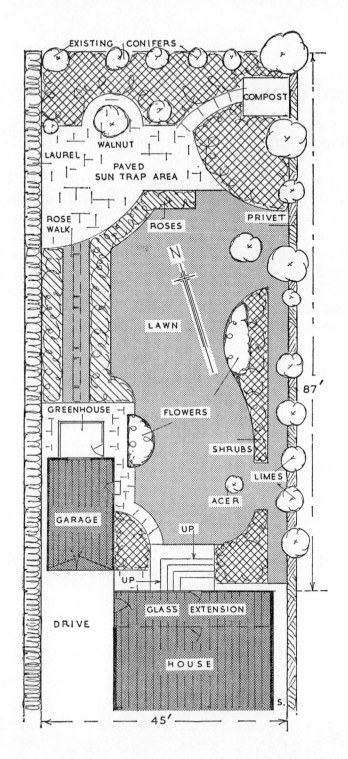

EXISTING CONIFERS

COMPOST

WALNUT

LAUREL

PAVED
SUN TRAP AREA

PRIVET

ROSE
WALK

ROSES

N

LAWN

GREENHOUSE

FLOWERS

SHRUBS

LIMES

GARAGE

ACER

UP

UP

DRIVE

GLASS EXTENSION

HOUSE

87′

45′

S.

Beside a stream
MAIDSTONE, KENT

This unusual plot has a stream and grass bank flanking the whole length of the east side. A 1 ft. 6 in. high wall marks the boundary, and the plot slopes slightly from north to south.

It is possible to make a charming garden on such a site, but there is difficulty in obtaining some privacy without obstructing the views.

A level lawn is planned, based on the position of two existing small trees on the bank of the stream. These give slight screening to the path which encircles the lawn and links with the kitchen door. The necessary retaining wall is recessed near the bungalow to give room for temporary seating, facing east. There is a view from here upstream. The foreground is brightened by low flower planting in long troughs or shallow bowls. Prickly subjects such as berberis and climbing roses are planted on the garden side of the low east boundary wall to clothe the top of it, without obstructing the view.

Steps in the retaining wall lead up to an oval lawn. This slopes slightly up to a permanent seat, set on paving and well recessed amongst shrubs in the north corner. From this fairly private, very sunny spot there is a view down and across the stream.

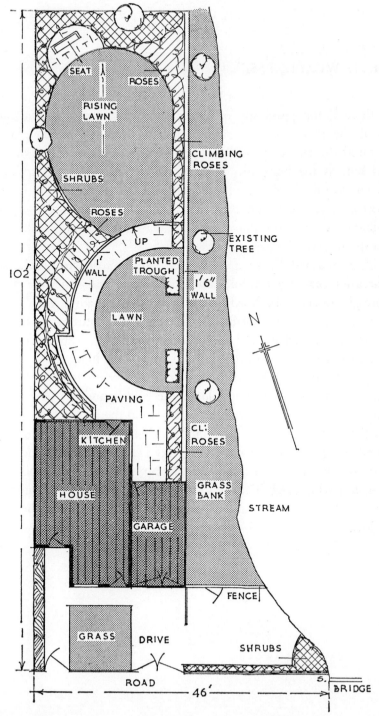

SEAT

ROSES

RISING
LAWN

SHRUBS

ROSES

CLIMBING
ROSES

EXISTING
TREE

UP

WALL

PLANTED
TROUGH

1'6"
WALL

LAWN

N

PAVING

KITCHEN

CL:
ROSES

GRASS
BANK

HOUSE

STREAM

GARAGE

FENCE

GRASS DRIVE

SHRUBS

ROAD

46'

S.

BRIDGE

102

A brook in the garden
NORTH WEALD, ESSEX

This small bungalow garden has high, closed fencing on two sides, but there is the possibility of bringing a small brook, at the north end of the plot, into the garden picture. None of the neighbours had faced the challenge and had fenced off the last few feet of their plots but, as the bungalow faced north, it seemed worth trying to incorporate this rather derelict section into the garden.

Fortunately, the brook runs across the plot at an angle, so it is possible to widen it out into a pool and leave room in the south corner for a slightly raised, paved area for a seat.

This is reached by stepping stones which cross the brook, skirt an area for planting primulas and similar bog and waterside plants, before giving access back across the brook to the main lawn.

Curved borders for shrubs clothe the stark outlines of the side fencing, and an island bed for perennials or low shrubs is colourful as seen from the seat and the sliding doors of the bungalow.

A paved area outside the doors is outlined with roses, and a firm path leads from the paving, down the east boundary, past a large grouping of flowers, towards the seat beyond the brook.

In the front garden, the drive allows plenty of room for movement around the garage and front door. A bold planting of rhododendrons stands out banked up behind a retaining wall, while heathers give colour at paving level. The addition of a lamp makes this a functional front garden, very pleasant at all seasons as seen from the study window.

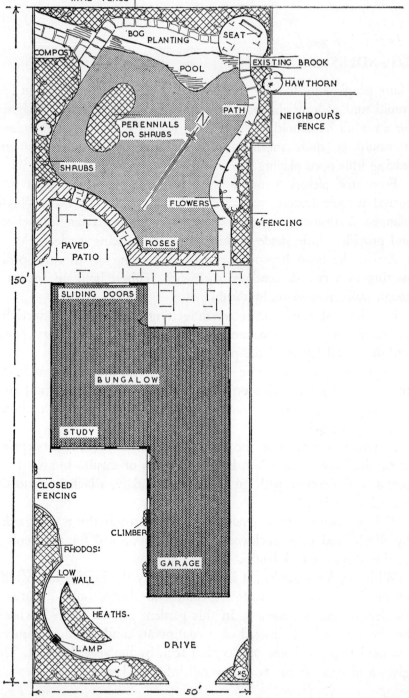

WIRE FENCE

BOG PLANTING

SEAT

COMPOST

EXISTING BROOK

POOL

HAWTHORN

PERENNIALS
OR SHRUBS

PATH

NEIGHBOUR'S
FENCE

SHRUBS

FLOWERS

6'FENCING

PAVED
PATIO

ROSES

150'

SLIDING DOORS

BUNGALOW

STUDY

CLOSED
FENCING

CLIMBER

RHODOS:

LOW
WALL

GARAGE

HEATHS.

LAMP

DRIVE

50'

145

Artificial pools
THUNDERSLEY, ESSEX

Many people long to have an informal pool in their garden, but few would find such an elaborate layout as this practical. It was designed for an adult household to enjoy from the large picture window, and it would be quite unsuitable for children, being dangerous and leaving little open playing space.

From the picture window there is a view over the lawn to a curved pergola feature, with a seat and screening rose beds. This is planned to frame the garden view, take off the rectangular effect, and provide a little shade in this sunny, south-facing garden.

Across the lawn beyond the roses is a string of informal pools, starting as a cascade amongst rockwork. This is built up against a rough wall screened out by shrubs.

For the best results it is worth getting advice from a specialist in water garden construction on the siting of the necessary pump and the actual layout of the pools and linking streams.

Stepping stones lead from the pergola across the stream and continue as a flagstone edge on the west side of the water until they cross the stream again to lead to a summer house, set into a curved boundary shrub border.

A paved terrace near the house has corner steps, and stepping stones lead across the lawn, between groups of shrubs, to give direct access to the service path on the west boundary, which leads to the vegetable garden.

This is enclosed by a fence and screened from the water garden by shrubs and more rockwork. The soil excavated for the pools is used to shape the rock banks.

With any long garden, it is a help to vary the heights and widths of the boundary treatments. A continuous hedge only accentuates the length and narrowness. In this garden, privacy is needed badly on the west side so, instead of a continuous conifer hedge, climbers are used near the house and cordon fruit by the vegetable plot. This gives a pleasing frame to the overall informal layout.

146

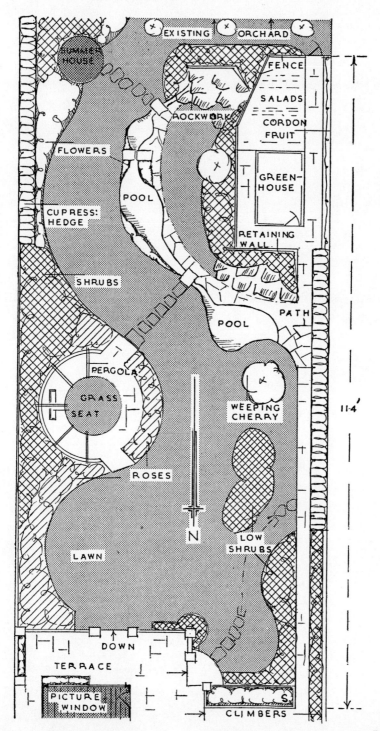

EXISTING ORCHARD

FENCE

SALADS

CORDON FRUIT

SUMMER HOUSE

ROCKWORK

FLOWERS

GREEN-HOUSE

POOL

CUPRESS: HEDGE

RETAINING WALL

SHRUBS

PATH

POOL

PERGOLA

GRASS SEAT

WEEPING CHERRY

11·4'

ROSES

N

LOW SHRUBS

LAWN

DOWN

TERRACE

PICTURE WINDOW

S

CLIMBERS

147

8 Leisure gardens

Gardening should be fun. Not just a yearly round of routine jobs, or a feeling all the time that you will never catch up on the weeds. Sensible planning and planting can ensure that all the family have energy and space to enjoy all sorts of leisure-time activities.

New gardens can be laid out so that maintenance work is cut to a minimum, and old-established gardens can be re-arranged. Any alterations you can make to the garden layout to bring it into line with your present needs makes the unavoidable work of maintenance more interesting and worth while. Why mow a large lawn you don't really need when you would much rather look at gay groupings of flowering shrubs underplanted with permanent ground cover?

As the family grows, the space given to swing and climbing frame can become a barbecue area. The sand pit can become a formal or informal pool, set in that sunny corner of the garden where it is now possible to relax on summer afternoons. Perhaps it is time to make room for the greenhouse or frames, seat or summerhouse you have always wanted.

Gardens, although on average smaller than in the past, are once again becoming places where all age groups expect to find relaxation and entertainment. A swimming pool is no longer just a pipe dream for the owner of a small garden. It is a possibility. Enthusiasts are finding space for miniature golf, croquet, badminton, tennis and even cricket practice nets. Modern materials make it possible for the garden to become a real extension of the home by, in many ways, beating out unpredictable weather.

Transparent roofing materials give gay protection without costly maintenance. Decorative fencing, screen walling and container planting give immediate privacy, if desired. Weather-proof and easily stored equipment is available, and the wide range of furniture which can be used indoors or out is making the barbecue area, dining recess or restful patio the delight of many families. The final touch of lighting makes entertaining as easy outdoors as in the house.

149

This worth-while trend is helping to bring house and garden together as a working unit, which the whole family circle can enjoy in their leisure hours—leaving the crowded motorways to others less fortunate.

Labour-saving alterations
SEVEN KINGS, ESSEX

The wide flower borders across the rear of this house were very difficult to keep tidy and, as the land rises slightly from the house, tended to block the main view from the picture window.

The long path dividing the plot into two equal parts made the garden very uninteresting and spoiled the graceful effect of the existing apple trees. Wide flower borders on the side boundaries were unwieldy, and the straight borders flanking the path from the patio made the use of the clothes drier very awkward.

The view from the patio is improved by making a circle of paving, wide enough to accommodate the drier with ease. This is outlined by low dry walls, backed by narrow borders for matt-growing alpines. Rose beds, following the line of the low wall, are backed by the apple trees, now standing free on the lawn. Two ways up to the main lawn, near the patio, as well as from the circle, make for much easier access to the garden.

The borders across the rear of the house are now reduced in width, and planted with low-growing hybrid tea roses. These bring colour to the picture window without obstructing the distant view of the garden.

The east boundary border is reshaped to be more interesting as seen from the picture window. It is planted with labour-saving shrubs, but allows room for growing a few favourite perennials. A paved edging to this section of the border makes for easy maintenance at all times.

The west boundary border is narrowed down to give room only for climbers on the fence, and bulbs and ground-cover planting at their base. The retained vegetable garden is now screened by a cheerful hedge of *Prunus cistena* 'Crimson Dwarf'.

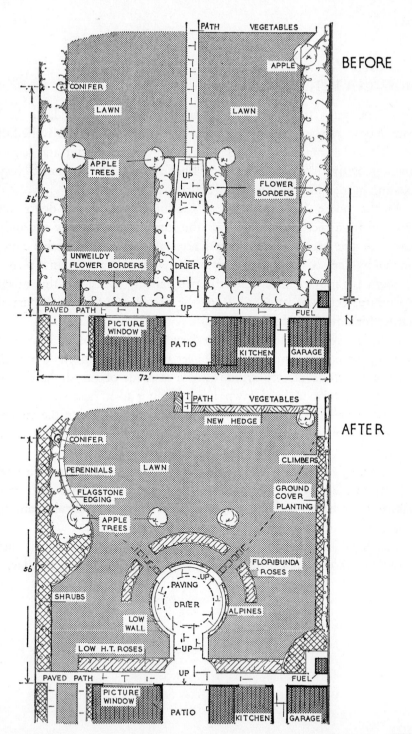

BEFORE

PATH VEGETABLES

APPLE

CONIFER

LAWN LAWN

56'

APPLE TREES

UP PAVING

FLOWER BORDERS

UNWEILDY FLOWER BORDERS

DRIER

UP

N

PAVED PATH

FUEL

PICTURE WINDOW

PATIO

KITCHEN GARAGE

72'

AFTER

PATH VEGETABLES

NEW HEDGE

CONIFER

PERENNIALS

LAWN

CLIMBERS

FLAGSTONE EDGING

GROUND COVER PLANTING

APPLE TREES

FLORIBUNDA ROSES

56'

SHRUBS

PAVING

DRIER

ALPINES

LOW WALL

UP

LOW H.T. ROSES

UP

PAVED PATH

UP

FUEL

PICTURE WINDOW

PATIO

KITCHEN GARAGE

151

Planned for retirement
HORNCHURCH, ESSEX

For some years this odd-shaped plot had just a central lawn and boundary shrub and flower borders. The pear tree fruited well, but was felt to be something of a liability with scattered fruit and leaves making cultivation of the border rather difficult. It was not a very exciting garden in which to spend retirement.

As the house faces north-west, the little-used french doors are replaced by a picture window. As the kitchen door is now the only access to the garden, an enlarged area of paving is included here, linked by the existing paths with a new paved area giving plenty of room for movement around the two existing sheds. All this tidied up utility section is screened from the picture window by a curved border for flowering shrubs.

A wide sweep to the south boundary shrub border ends in a bold planting of flowers and gives the effect of a private, intimate garden as seen from the picture window. Use is made of the slight rise in the land to form a level lawn here, leading to a raised terrace set across the garden, facing south. There are two ways up to the terrace from the main lawn and another from the new paved area by the sheds.

A low, coped wall, backed by a narrow flower border gives a neat dignity to the garden. The pear tree now stands on the paved terrace where it can be pruned and tended as a specimen tree. Shrub planting to the west and south gives privacy to the terrace.

The new arrangements make for an interesting, convenient and easily run garden. One which can be enjoyed at any time of the day.

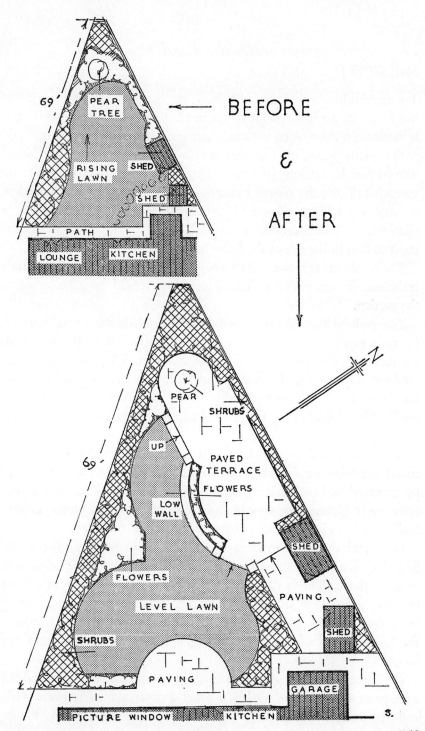

BEFORE

&

AFTER

69'

PEAR
TREE

RISING
LAWN

SHED

SHED

PATH

LOUNGE   KITCHEN

N

69'

PEAR

SHRUBS

UP

PAVED
TERRACE

FLOWERS

LOW
WALL

FLOWERS

SHED

PAVING

LEVEL LAWN

SHED

SHRUBS

PAVING

GARAGE

PICTURE WINDOW   KITCHEN

S.

153

A garden grows with the family
SHENFIELD, ESSEX

Young children and those of school age expect little from a garden but an open, uncluttered lawn where all sorts of ball games and other activities can take place without damaging surrounding plants.

For many years, this garden had a few flowers near the house. Ten-foot-high netting protected them and the glass roof of the verandah during the summer months. With narrow boundary borders, a large vegetable garden and two apple trees large enough to be climbed, the whole arrangement made a dull-looking, but very useful contribution to the life of the household.

Then, about the time that the nursery finally became a study bedroom, it was realised that different use could now be made of the garden.

The path by the kitchen door is now extended into a small terrace, giving a much more ample way down from the house. The rose beds are rearranged to outline a small square lawn. This forms a natural outdoor play-pen for the first grandchild. It is overlooked by a seat, set on paving. This unexpectedly large sitting out place was made possible by demolishing the fuel shed, made redundant by central heating.

As the old willow tree had died, there is room for a shed and paved extension outside the rear door of the garage. This is screened by a curved bed for azaleas, giving colour near the house before the roses are in bloom. The west boundary flower border is now enlarged, and curved to give a circular shape to the end of the lawn.

Trees and shrubs planted to screen new buildings beyond the east boundary have now grown so high that this part of the garden is in deep shade. The border has been abandoned to spring woodland flowers, and a new island shrub border cut out of the lawn, away from deep shadow and tree roots. This makes a pleasant way round the lawn instead of seeing the whole garden at a glance from the house.

The large vegetable garden is no longer needed, so flowers and a wide grass walk replace all but a small section of it. The grass walk leads between two espalier pears planted across the garden. Black-

A FAMILY GARDEN   FIFTEEN YEARS LATER

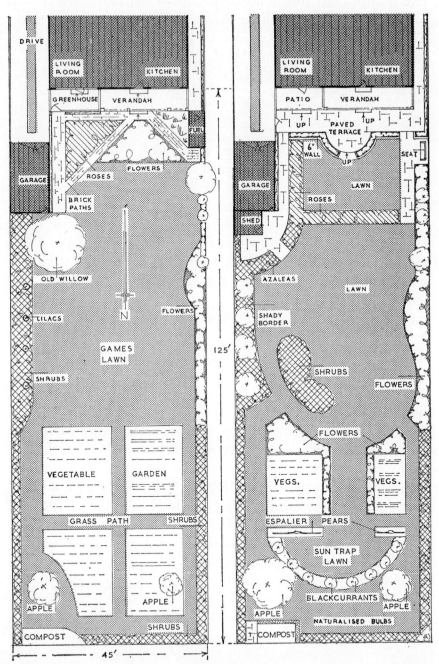

155

currant bushes, planted in a semi-circle, combine with the pears to give a small lawn area, completely secluded and in full sun all day, away from the deep afternoon shade cast by the north-facing house. The two apple trees, now surrounded by grass and naturalised bulbs, still make a restful background to the garden.

A swimming pool in a small garden
UPMINSTER, ESSEX

The plan of this garden is geared to the needs of a family of boys. Together they dug out the site for the swimming pool, and then called in expert help to advise them on the actual pool and the best way to blend it with the rest of the garden.

Existing flowering trees and the fine background of conifers help to soften the general effect. A low wall, one foot high, keeps soil in the boundary borders away from the paving surrounding the swimming pool, and this also gives room for planting small spring bulbs, followed by neat summer bedding.

An eighteen-inch coped wall on the west side of the pool provides handy sitting space, and an existing shed is adapted as a changing room. The coped wall is backed by shrubs, two to three feet high, making a decorative break between the lawn and swimming pool. The main lawn is kept open, as a general games area. There is room here for badminton.

A narrow flower border, facing south, is outlined by a paved path for tidy maintenance, and to give direct dry access from the kitchen to the pool. The existing shrub border facing north is made more interesting by forming a recess between two existing trees to allow room for a seat, for players awaiting their turn.

Colour and interest is brought into view from the living-room windows by incorporating rose beds in a small paved area, shaped to allow room for meals out of doors.

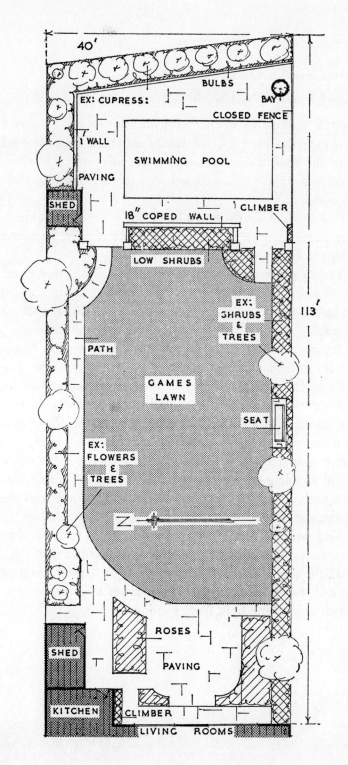

40'

BULBS

EX: CUPRESS:

BAY

CLOSED FENCE

1 WALL

SWIMMING POOL

PAVING

SHED

CLIMBER

18" COPED WALL

LOW SHRUBS

113'

EX: SHRUBS & TREES

PATH

GAMES LAWN

SEAT

EX: FLOWERS & TREES

N

ROSES

SHED

PAVING

KITCHEN

CLIMBER

LIVING ROOMS

157

Planned for a young family
MATCHING GREEN, ESSEX

The sensible positioning of the house on this plot allows ample room for developing several areas for family activities. From the existing paving by the kitchen door, a curved path leads past a colourful shrub bed to leave a small grass or paved area for a swing, in view of the kitchen window.

The path leads along the north boundary, where the old field hedge has been trimmed back to allow for glimpses of open farmland from the various windows of the house.

The far corner, facing south, is developed as a barbecue area and sitting out place. The whole area is raised up by utilising soil from the sunken lawn. The varying levels add interest to this flat site, as seen from the study window.

The retaining wall of the barbecue area is used as a background for a fountain jet and informal pools. The garden is to be developed gradually by the owner, and the various water features will probably not be achieved until the youngest child is at least of school age.

Space is found for a shaped swimming pool at the side of the house, and its outlining paving is softened by beds for low-growing shrubs. A decorative seven-foot wall gives privacy from the front garden and drive, and double gates screen an extra car standing place, which also makes a useful hard surface play area in conjunction with the lawn area in the east corner.

Weeping willows seem to be prime favourites with the owners of small gardens, but in this case, planted in association with the decorative wall, the tree gives a softening effect to the large expanse of drive and privacy to the side garden. It has room to grow without being mutilated, or blocking light from windows.

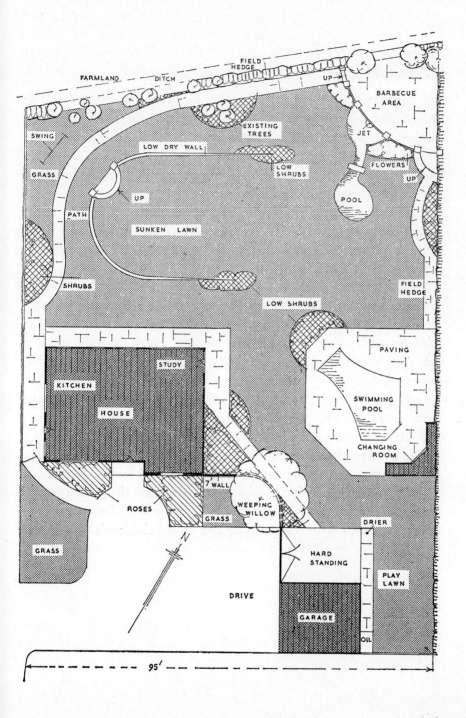

A corner retreat
ILFORD, ESSEX

The main view of this garden is from the sun room extension. The immediate need was for extra paving to give room for movement. The existing paving was extended into a semi-circle and outlined with flowers. To bring these into more direct view from the sun room windows the beds were raised up in trough walls. This had the added advantage of keeping loose soil away from the paving.

The existing path is retained to lead to the north-east corner, where paving replaces unsatisfactory planting under the two existing fruit trees. A permanent seat here provides a retreat from the children's activities on the main lawn.

To give greater seclusion, a semi-circular low wall is built, enclosing a small lawn and flower beds. The wall forms a background for a rock bank sloping down to the lawn, and means that the owner can fulfil his wish to grow alpines effectively, although his garden site is flat. A flagstone edge, or a soil gully, soon covered by overhanging alpines, makes for easy maintenance of the lawn.

Low-growing roses, backed by climbing roses, fill the border on the north boundary, and the whole arrangement brings the main colour and interest of the garden into view from the sun room.

The existing conifer hedge is continued round towards the south boundary to screen a shed and the compost area. A bed for floribunda roses in front of the hedge is colourful as seen from the seat. A curved border for shrubs screens the existing path up the south boundary. Two existing apple trees are left standing free on the children's play lawn.

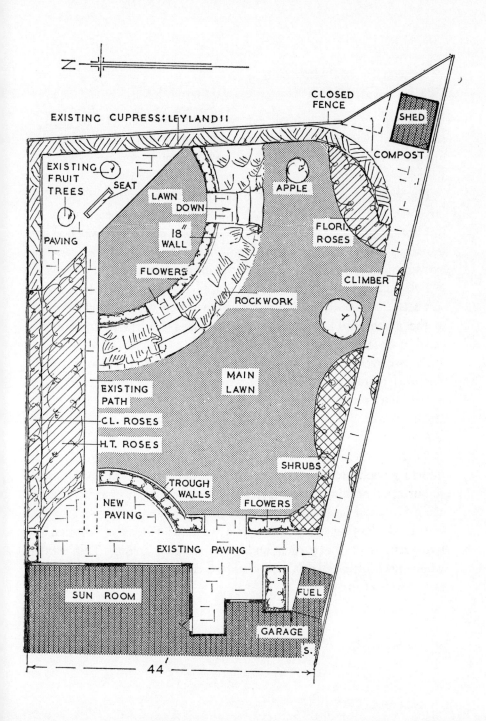

N

EXISTING CUPRESS: LEYLAND!!

CLOSED
FENCE

SHED

COMPOST

EXISTING
FRUIT
TREES

SEAT

LAWN
DOWN

APPLE

18"
WALL

FLORI.
ROSES

PAVING

FLOWERS

CLIMBER

ROCKWORK

MAIN
LAWN

EXISTING
PATH

CL. ROSES

H.T. ROSES

SHRUBS

TROUGH
WALLS

NEW
PAVING

FLOWERS

EXISTING PAVING

SUN ROOM

FUEL

GARAGE

S.

44'

161

An 'easy-care' garden
UPMINSTER, ESSEX

In a small, enclosed garden, constructional materials can be used in association with carefully chosen planting to give a labour-saving garden which is satisfying at all seasons. It may be possible to dispense with lawn altogether.

This small space is planned so that it cannot be seen at a glance. The large ash tree makes plant growth difficult in the north-east corner, so this area is paved. However, space is left for a circular flower bed and a shaped shrub border away from overhanging branches, and an existing path leaves room for flower planting against the house walls.

This path links with a wide semi-circle of paving, with space for a seat set facing south-west. Five-foot-high screen walling backs the seat to the north, and continues along the east boundary in front of the existing closed fencing.

The seat recess could be level with a central lawn, but if paving is used instead of grass it would be worth while raising the recess a few inches, and using coloured paving as a contrast to the main paved areas.

A rough, low retaining wall in the south-east corner allows for a soil bank planted with shrubs, as a background to rockwork and an informal pool. Heath plantings towards the front of the border give colour at all seasons. Their softening effect would be especially useful against a paved outline.

A bold planting of roses makes a permanent division between the two sections of the garden and gives summer colour. This garden would need little upkeep, and could be enjoyed on an odd sunny day at any time of the year.

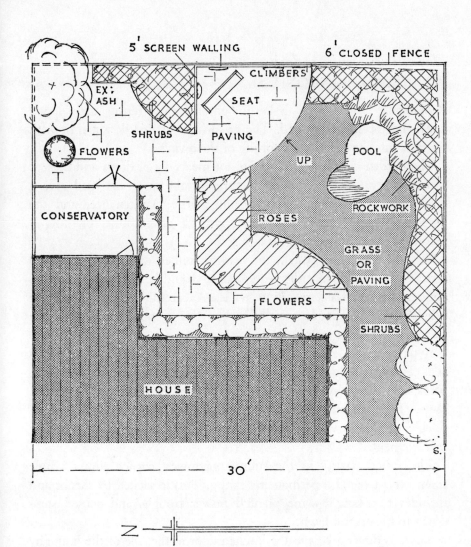

5' SCREEN WALLING
6' CLOSED FENCE
CLIMBERS
EX:
ASH
SEAT
SHRUBS
PAVING
FLOWERS
UP
POOL
ROCKWORK
CONSERVATORY
ROSES
GRASS
OR
PAVING
FLOWERS
SHRUBS
HOUSE
S.

30'

N

163

A labour-saving design
WANSTEAD, LONDON E.11

A haphazard old garden makes an unsatisfactory setting for a house which has been modernised. The crisp lines of this design link with the new interior and the way of life of the owners.

The garden now has ample room for meals out of doors and there is a barbecue area. The varying textures of the materials used give a decorative effect at all times, needing little maintenance, and the garden is ready for use at the first glimpse of sunshine. Planting is mainly of labour-saving shrubs and roses.

To save even more work, the central sunken area could be paved instead of grassed. In either case cobbles could be used, as shown, to outline the necessary retaining walls. A careful watering over the cobbles with a suitable weedkiller in spring, would deal with the weeding here for a season.

A paved patio is brought up to the level of the new sliding doors and continues as a path along the south boundary to the barbecue. Steps lead down by the house and from the barbecue to the central lawn. The sweeping rose border linking the steps is contained in double retaining walls, giving a neat effect and making for easy management.

The raised paving in the sunny north-west corner allows ample room for a table and permanent seating. This is backed by shrubs and includes two lamps, some planted flower troughs and curved steps down to the central lawn.

There is direct access to the kitchen door at the side of the house by means of a path between shrub and flower borders, leading through a gate in the fencing which screens out the utility area. The kitchen door and sliding doors are linked by paving across the back of the house, made colourful by shallow flower bowls, set on cobbles.

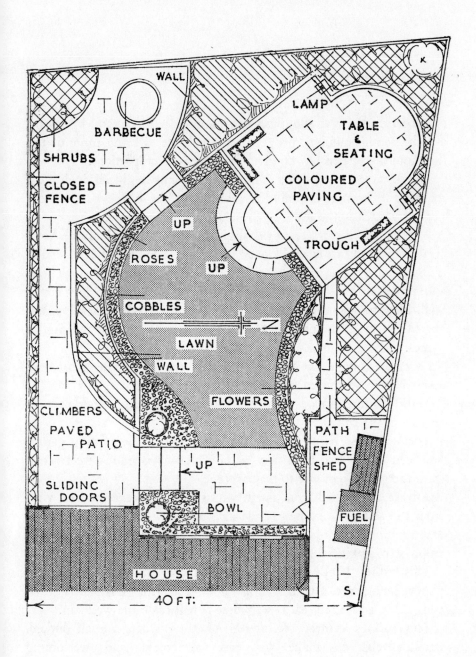

WALL

BARBECUE

SHRUBS

CLOSED
FENCE

LAMP

TABLE
&
SEATING

COLOURED
PAVING

TROUGH

UP

ROSES

UP

COBBLES

LAWN

WALL

FLOWERS

CLIMBERS

PAVED
PATIO

PATH

FENCE
SHED

SLIDING
DOORS

UP

BOWL

FUEL

HOUSE

40 FT:

S.

165

Planned for entertaining
HARLOW, ESSEX

This old cottage, built along the roadside, had only forty feet depth of garden at the rear. Building extensions were made, and by taking out the south boundary hedge, it was possible to bring more of the field into the garden layout, giving much better proportions.

The cottage is set down below the existing eighteen inch wall retaining a lawn area, and the removal of the hedge gave a very necessary extension to the view from the cottage windows.

A new, paved terrace, raised slightly above the level of the lawn area, commands wide views over farmland. The terrace is extended into a semi-circle to allow room for a built-in barbecue area, floodlit and protected by low, wrought-iron balustrading on the low coped wall. New tree plantings frame the view of the garden extension, but apart from these, the new lawn area is left free for croquet and similar games.

From the cottage, the two side doors of the main living room give access onto a wide area of sheltered paving, with plenty of room for garden furniture. Azaleas and heaths give permanent colour here, as seen from the cottage.

The wide rose border against the south side of the existing garage has been cut in two by a new path, which gives more direct access from the garage entrance to the barbecue.

An area, protected from north winds by the garages and on view from the cottage windows, is left as a play lawn for young children, and additional paving to the north side of the garages ends in broad, ample steps linking the old and new parts of the garden.

This rather windy corner is made more convenient for tennis players by a pergola, with seating under, and with glass panels at the ends. Also, a recessed seat is set where it will catch the west sun.

The various centres of interest of the garden are all linked, unobtrusively, to make for easy movement and welcoming accommodation of visitors.

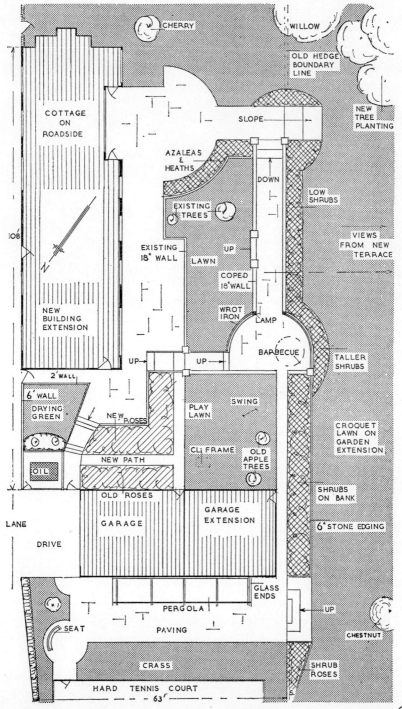

CHERRY

WILLOW

OLD HEDGE
BOUNDARY
LINE

COTTAGE
ON
ROADSIDE

NEW
TREE
PLANTING

SLOPE

AZALEAS
&
HEATHS

DOWN

LOW
SHRUBS

EXISTING
TREES

108

EXISTING
18" WALL

LAWN

UP

VIEWS
FROM NEW
TERRACE

NEW
BUILDING
EXTENSION

COPED
18" WALL

WROT
IRON

LAMP

UP →

UP →

BARBECUE

TALLER
SHRUBS

2' WALL

6' WALL

DRYING
GREEN

NEW ROSES

PLAY
LAWN

SWING

CROQUET
LAWN ON
GARDEN
EXTENSION

OIL

NEW PATH

CL. FRAME

OLD
APPLE
TREES

OLD ROSES

SHRUBS
ON BANK

LANE

GARAGE

GARAGE
EXTENSION

6' STONE EDGING

DRIVE

GLASS
ENDS

UP →

SEAT

PERGOLA

PAVING

CHESTNUT

CRASS

SHRUB
ROSES

HARD   TENNIS   COURT
- - 63' - -

167

Index